Real Time Programming

Programming

Neglected Topics

Real Time Programming

Neglected Topics

Caxton C. Foster
University of Massachusetts

ADDISON-WESLEY PUBLISHING COMPANY
Reading, Massachusetts · Menlo Park, California
London · Amsterdam · Don Mills, Ontario · Sydney

This book is in the
Addison-Wesley series in **The Joy of Computing**

Thomas A. Dwyer, *Consulting Editor*

Library of Congress Cataloging in Publication Data

Foster, Caxton C.   1929-
  Real time programming.

  (Addison-Wesley series in joy of computing)
  Includes index.
  1. Real-time data processing.   2.   Electronic
digital computers—Programming.
II.   Title.
QA76 54.F67   001.644'04   80-20395
ISBN 0-201-01937-X

ISBN 0-201-01937-X
ABCDEFGHIJ-AL-8987654321

To Bill and Anatol

He isn't actually out of touch with reality.
He just chooses to ignore it!

Anonymous

Preface

This book is about some of the problems you will run up against if you try to connect a digital computer to the real world. It is more a survey of these problems than it is a collection of cookbook recipes for solution of the problems. By the time you finish reading this book and doing the experiments described herein, you will begin to have an appreciation of all the things you don't know and we didn't know how to tell you. Part of the reason for this open-endedness is the fact that we are going to consider enough topics to make up the better part of a full-fledged masters program in electrical engineering or computer science. We will look at simple interrupts and hierarchical interrupts. Semaphores (on which one well-known author spends almost 80 pages) we will "cover" in less than 10, counting illustrations. We will examine ports, PIAs, and timers, which are standard hardware devices for connecting a CPU to the outside world. We will talk about analog-to-digital and digital-to-analog converters, about the sampling theorem, and about digital filters, each of which could consume the better part of a semester by itself.

Having waded through all that, we will then attack closed loop control systems—elementary feedback, derivative and integral control, nonlinear servos, bang-bang systems, and then for good measure, we will mention optimal and adaptive control systems.

Finally, we will look at various forms of multiplexing, at buses and communication, and at distributed computer systems.

It should be obvious without our needing to belabor the point that no book less than 10 inches thick could cover all these topics in detail. So what are we doing? We are trying to introduce the topics that you had better know something about if you want to consider yourself an expert on computers. If you never read another word on one of these topics, at least you won't be at a total loss if somebody starts talking about time-division multiplexing, or error-rate control.

One way we have used to condense these topics is to leave out most of the mathematics. In the discussion of filters and feedback control, we have had to include some differential equations, but we have tried very hard to make them auxiliary to the text rather than central, and they can be skipped over without undue loss. In keeping with this avoidance of mathematics, we have eschewed all use of complex numbers. Our feeling was that not one student in ten would have profited from their inclusion, and not one computer hobbyist in a hundred would have the energy or the background to follow them.

We have taught the course called "Real Time Programming" twice at the University of Massachusetts, and this book is the result of our experience. The course is offered to sophomores and juniors as a third course in computer science after a course in Fortran and one in assembly-language programming. The course is intended for computer science majors and is probably all that most of them will ever see of most of these topics. Some will be turned on by one or another and will pursue it in later years, but most will, of course, turn the last page with a sigh of relief and pray that they never have to hear of any of them again.

Computer hobbyists will perhaps have more need of this book than will students in a more formal situation. There is, as far as we know, no other source (or sources) that hobbyists can turn to that even attempt to treat these topics on a practical level. Any good technical library will have shelves full of books on each of the topics we treat so rapidly here, but unfortunately many of those texts are not very comprehensible.

Amherst, Massachusetts   C.C.F.
May 1981

Contents

1 Basic Interrupts

In this chapter we are going to examine the ways that have been developed that allow a computer to respond rapidly to external events while at the same time permitting the machine to do other useful work. We need to look because in many real world situations there exist several external events that must be monitored, and in other cases the machine must do some calculation based on previous events so that it can take certain actions when a particular pattern is detected.

POLLING

Let us consider first an extremely simple case that scarcely justifies the use of a computer at all. Assume that the XYZ Manufacturing Company produces widgets and packs them 144 to a box. Our task is to count the number of widgets passing the final assembly line station and ring a bell to alert the packer to move a new box under the end of the line every time 144 widgets have gone by. Figure 1.1 shows the

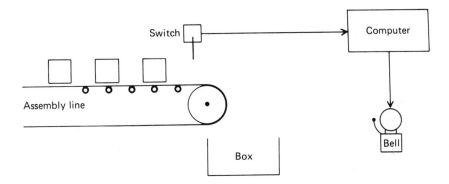

Figure 1.1 *The widget assembly line counter.*

1

```
         INIT:   LDAIM   0
                 STA     COUNT        Clear counter to zero.
         LOOP:   INPUT   SWITCH       0 = open, 1 = closed.
                 BZA     LOOP         Wait for switch to close.
                 LDA     COUNT
                 ADDIM   1
                 STA     COUNT        Add 1 to count.
                 SUBIM   144
                 BMA     LOOP         Is the box full?
                 LDAIM   1
                 OUTPUT  BELL         Yes, ring the bell.
                 LDAIM   0
                 STA     COUNT        Zero the count.
                 LDAIM   0
                 STA     BELL         Turn off the bell.
                 JMP     LOOP         Do it again.
```

Figure 1.2 *The FOSSOL program for the widget counter.*

situation in abstract form. Every time a widget goes by, the switch is closed and the computer sensing the switch closure (we will see how it senses this later on) adds one to its count of "widgets in the box." When that count reaches 144, the computer will ring the bell, reset its count to zero and start over. Figure 1.2 shows a program to accomplish this task. The program is written in a language called "FOSSOL," which corresponds to no particular existing machine but which we have invented ad hoc with the features we need to discuss our various examples and problems. Appendix 1 contains a list of the op-codes and a brief description of the machine.

Now there are all kinds of things wrong with the program in Figure 1.2. We assumed that the switch closed for only a short period of time—long enough so we can detect that it was closed but not so long that we can detect it twice. We assumed that just a short signal to the bell would cause it to ring, and worst of all, we assumed that the packer was there and on top of his job and changing the box every time the bell rings. If he ever takes a coffee break, there are going to be widgets all over the floor.

Another assumption we made was that the switch used to detect widgets doesn't "bounce." Almost any physical (as opposed to ideal or theoretical) switch has what is called "contact bounce." This means that when it is first actuated, it will close, then open again, then close, then open, and so on, for several cycles extending over one or two milliseconds before it settles down to a good solid closure.* There are two ways to insure that switch bounce is not a problem. The easiest (for the programmer) is to buy switches that are electronically "debounced." But that costs money. The other way to solve the problem is to wait

---

*   Caxton C. Foster, *Programming a Microcomputer: 6502*, Addison-Wesley, Reading, MA, 1978.

INSTRUCTION EQUIVALENTS

Below is a table of *approximate* instruction equivalents for FOSSOL, the 6502, and the Z-80. Often there are other and better ways of accomplishing the same result. Where no single equivalent exists we have suggested short strings of instructions that do about the same thing.

FOSSOL		6502			Z-80			
LDA	α	LDA	α		LD	A,(α)		
LDX	α	LDX	α		LD	IX,(α)		
LSP	α	LDX	α	TXS	LD	HL,(α)	LD	SP,HL
ADD	α	CLC	ADC	α	LD	HL,α	ADD	A,(HL)
SUB	α	SEC	SBC	α	LD	HL,α	SUB	(HL)
AND	α	AND	α		LD	HL,α	AND	(HL)
IOR	α	ORA	α		LD	H,α	OR	(HL)
STA	α	STA	α		LD	(α),A		
INC	α	INC	α		LD	HL,α	INC	(HL)
DEC	α	DEC	α		LD	HL,α	DEC	(HL)
JMP	α	JMP	α		JP	α		
JSR	α	JSR	α		CALL	α		
BZA	α	BEQ	α		JP	Z,α		
BPA	α	BPL	α		JP	P,α		
BNA	α	BNE	α		JP	N,α		
BMA	α	BMI	α		JP	M,α		
INPUT	α	LDA	α		IN	A,(α)		
OUTPUT	α	STA	α		OUT	(α),A		
SEI		SEI			DI			
CLI		CLI			EI			
RTS		RTS			RET			
RTI		RTI			RETI			
HLT		——			HALT			
INX		INX			INC	IX		
ASR		LSR	$(m \geqslant 0)$		SRA	A		
TXA		TXA			LD	A,IX		
TAX		TAX			LD	IX,A		
PUSHA		PHA			LD	IX,A	PUSH	IX
PUSHX		TXA	PHA		PUSH	IX		
POPA		PLA			POP	IX	LD	A,X
POPX		PLA	TAX		POP	IX		

until any possible switch bounce is over. When we detect a switch closure (or opening), we do whatever we need to do, and before we come back to test the switch again, we enter a delay loop that "wastes" perhaps 3 milliseconds and then test the switch again.

Figure 1.3 shows a modified set up, and Figure 1.4 shows the program to go with it. First of all, we have added a button for the packer to push to tell the com-

FIRST WIDGET COUNTER PROGRAM
for a 6502 and a Z-80

Just as an example of how it is done, we have translated the FOSSOL program of Figure 1.4 into real machine language. We assume SWITCH is an input port and BELL is an output port. We keep the count in index register X.

	6502			Z-80	
INIT:	LDXIM	0	INIT:	LD	IX,0
LOOP:	LDA	SWITCH	LOOP:	IN	A,(SWITCH)
	BEQ	LOOP		JP	Z,LOOP
	INX			INC	IX
	CPX	144		LD	A,IX
	BMI	LOOP		CP	144
	LDAIM	1		JP	M,LOOP
	STA	BELL		LD	A,1
	LDAIM	0		OUT	(BELL),A
	STA	BELL		LD	A,0
	JMP	INIT		OUT	(BELL),A
COUNT:	.BYT	0		JP	INIT
			COUNT:	.BYT	0

puter that he has changed the box, and second, we have added an output line from the computer that can stop and start the assembly line. This time we test to make sure the widget is clear of the switch before we go back to LOOP so that we don't count the same widget twice. Next we turn on the bell and stop the line until the packer responds. Note that we don't have to debounce the packer's push button or wait for it to go back to zero again. We can be pretty sure that by the time another gross of widgets comes down the line, it will be back at a stable zero. But the packer might just tape down the button so he doesn't have to listen to the bell going off. If you mistrust your fellow man, maybe you had better debounce the packer's button and wait for it to clear to zero (after a one) before you stop the bell and start the line up again.

So, we now have a program that does what it is supposed to with reasonable efficiency and reasonable clarity. But on the other hand, we have tied up the computer completely. When it isn't actually counting, it is sitting around waiting for an input from the switch or the packer's button. Suppose we had something else that we wanted the computer to do. Perhaps we might want it to control other parts of the assembly line, or perhaps we might want it to be calculating the company's payroll. With the setup of Figure 1.3 we don't dare go off to do something else, because we might miss a widget if it comes down the line when the computer isn't looking. What we need is a method whereby when an event occurs (in our case, the switch closure), it catches the computer's attention. The computer can then stop its regular job and turn its attention to the external event. For example, the computer

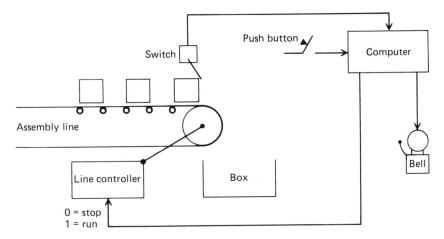

Figure 1.3 *Improved widget-packer station.*

INIT:	LDAIM	0	
	STA	COUNT	Clear the counter.
LOOP:	INPUT	SWITCH	
	BZA	LOOP	Wait for a switch closure.
	LDA	COUNT	
	ADDIM	1	
	STA	COUNT	Add 1 to count.
	SUBIM	144	
	BPA	CHANGEBOX	If count ≥ 144, change box.
	LDA	500	
D1:	SUBIM	1	Delay about 2 milliseconds to
	BPA	D1	debounce switch.
WAIT:	INPUT	SWITCH	
	BPA	WAIT	Wait for switch to open.
	LDA	500	
D2:	SUBIM	1	Delay about 2 milliseconds to
	BPA	D2	debounce switch.
	JMP	LOOP	
CHANGEBOX:	LDAIM	1	
	OUTPUT	BELL	Turn on the bell.
	LDAIM	0	
	OUTPUT	LINE	Stop the assembly line.
PUSH:	INPUT	BUTTON	
	BZA	PUSH	Wait for packer to respond.
	LDAIM	0	
	OUTPUT	BELL	Turn off the bell.
	LDAIM	1	
	OUTPUT	LINE	Start assembly line.
	JMP	INIT	

Figure 1.4 *Improved widget-packer program.*

might be busy doing the payroll, and when the widget counter switch detects another widget passing down the line, the switch somehow forces the computer to stop doing the payroll and transfer control to a routine that adds one to the widget count. Such an action is called an "interrupt."

SINGLE INTERRUPTS

Most computers have a line connected to the outside world called the "interrupt request" line, or IRQ for short. For reasons that need not concern us here, this line is very often what is called an "active low" line. That means that when you want to request an interrupt, you must put a logical zero (0 volts) on this line. When you *don't* want to request an interrupt, you put a logical one (+5 volts) on the line. Inside the computer there is a flip-flop called the "interrupt inhibit flip-flop," or "I-bit" for short. When this bit is one, interrupts are inhibited—that is, they are ignored. When the I-bit is zero, an interrupt request will be honored. The programmer may set or clear this bit with SEI and CLI instructions. If we liken an interrupt request to a phone call whose ringing drags you away from your present occupation, then the interrupt inhibit bit corresponds to the "muting" switch that prevents the bell from ringing.

Assume that the I-bit is zero (interrupts are permitted) and that an external device pulls the interrupt request line to zero (requests the attention of the CPU). Four things happen at this point in rapid succession:

1. The CPU finishes executing its present instruction (the one it was working on when the IRQ went to zero).
2. The present contents of the program counter (PC) are saved in some known storage location.
3. The interrupt inhibit bit is set to one.
4. The address of the interrupt-handling routine is loaded into the PC.

So much is true of all computers, but the details vary greatly from machine to machine. If the computer has a "stack," the old value of the PC (the address of the next instruction to be executed in the main or original program) is usually pushed onto the stack. If the computer has a PSW (processor status word containing various flags and often containing the I-bit), then usually (but not always) the PSW is also saved automatically on the stack along with the PC. For an 8080 or a Z-80 a simple interrupt will cause a zero to be loaded into the PC, forcing the computer to take its next instruction from location zero of the memory. For a 6502 there is a two-byte interrupt "vector" associated with the IRQ line, whose address may be discovered by reading your machine manual. When an interrupt comes along, the hardware automatically loads the contents of this vector into the PC, thus performing an indirect jump through the vector address. If a clever programmer has remembered to put the address of the interrupt-handling routine into the vector, then the next instruction that will be executed will be the first instruction of the interrupt-handling program. Some computers (the PDP-11, for example) have a two-word vector associated with each possible interrupt. One of these words holds

INTERRUPTS

6502

When an IRQ interrupt occurs in a 6502, the following operations take place at the end of the current instruction:

1. Store the PC high-order byte on the stack (page).
2. Store the PC low-order byte on the stack (line).
3. Store the PSW on the stack.
4. Turn ON the I-bit in the PSW.
5. Load PC high-order byte from memory location FFFF.
6. Load PC low-order byte from memory location FFFE.

Assuming the stackpointer contains FF before the interrupt: PCH → 01FF, PCL → 01FE, PSW → 01FD. Stackpointer contains FC.

At location FFFF and FFFE there is the address of a "jump indirect" instruction, which transfers control to the address stored in IRQVEC. Each computer using a 6502 puts IRQVEC in a different location, so see *your* machine manual for its actual address.

Z-80

A simple IRQ interrupt in the Z-80 causes the following operations to take place if the interrupt *enable* bit has been set:

1. The current instruction is completed.
2. The interrupt enable bit is cleared to 0, preventing further interrupts.
3. The CPU energizes the INTA (interrupt acknowledge) line, requesting the device to supply an instruction.
4. The device responds with a RST η (Restart at location 0000 + 8η).
5. The restart instruction causes the PC to be saved on the stack and then the PC to be loaded with 0000 + 8η.

The next instruction is taken from location 0000 + 8η, which should be the beginning of a routine to save context, including the PSW.

a new value for the PC (the address of the handling routine), and the other word holds a new value for the PSW. We will see why they wanted to do that later.

Our pseudomachine has a reserved location somewhere in storage (its actual address doesn't matter as long as both the hardware and the programmer can refer to it without ambiguity) called IRQVEC. When an interrupt on the IRQ line occurs, the contents of IRQVEC get loaded into the PC in step 4 above.

Figure 1.5 shows our widget counter redone using simple interrupts, and Figure 1.6 shows the revised connections of the switch. The program consists of three separate sections called INIT, MAIN, and HANDLER.

```
      INIT:     LDAIM      0
                STA        COUNT         Zero the count.
                LDAIM      HANDLER       Put the address of the interrupt
                STA        IRQVEC        handler into IRQVEC.
                CLI                      Turn off interrupt inhibit bit.
      MAIN:                              This is the main program, whose
                                         details we are not concerned with.
   HANDLER:     STA        SAVEA         Save the values in Acc and X so that
                STX        SAVEX         we can put them back later.
                LDA        COUNT
                ADDIM      1             Increment count by one.
                STA        COUNT
                SUBIM      144
                BPA        FULL          Box is full.
                                         (Delay here to debounce switch if
                                         required.)
      WAIT:     INPUT      SWITCH        Wait for widget to pass by.
                BZA        WAIT          Note inversion of switch relative to
                                         Program 1.4.
                                         (Delay if any danger of switch
                                         bouncing back to 0.)
                JMP        RESTORE
      FULL:     LDAIM      1             Ring bell.
                OUTPUT     BELL
                LDAIM      0             Stop assembly line.
                OUTPUT     LINE
                LDAIM      0             Clear count.
                STA        COUNT
   RESPONSE:    INPUT      BUTTON
                BZA        RESPONSE      Wait for packer's response.
                LDAIM      0             Turn off bell.
                OUTPUT     BELL
                LDAIM      1             Start assembly line.
                OUTPUT     LINE
   RESTORE:     LDA        SAVEA         Restore registers and return to main
                LDX        SAVEX         program.
                RTI
```

Figure 1.5 *Widget counter using interrupts.*

In INIT we store the address of the handler routine in IRQVEC so that when an interrupt comes along, the hardware will know where to transfer control to. Then we clear the I-bit so that interrupts can occur. Since we haven't specified what the main program is doing, the routine MAIN is left blank.

MAIN goes about its mysterious business, and sooner or later a widget comes down the line and causes the switch to output a zero. Since the I-bit is zero (interrupts are permitted), and since IRQ is now zero, the computer finishes its present

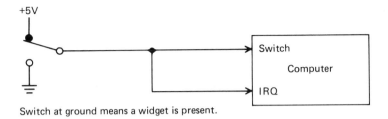

Switch at ground means a widget is present.

Figure 1.6 *Revised connections for interrupts by the widget switch.*

instruction, which we will assume was taken from cell β. Then the hardware built into the computer automatically saves the contents of the PC on the stack. Since the last instruction came from location β, the PC is pointing at $\beta + 1$, so that number gets pushed onto the stack. Next the I-bit gets set to one, so no other interrupts can occur, and then the hardware takes the number stored in IRQVEC and puts it in the PC and then goes back to its normal "fetch execute" cycle so that the next instruction to be executed by the machine is taken, not from $\beta + 1$ as would have been the case had no interrupt occurred, but from HANDLER. Notice that the hardware didn't know where the interrupt-processing routine (HANDLER) was stored, but it knew where to find out; namely, IRQVEC. Since we had remembered to put the address of HANDLER into IRQVEC during the initialization routine, it all worked out properly.

Now let us look at the details of HANDLER since it has changed from the program presented in Figure 1.4. The first thing we do is preserve the values we find in the accumulator and the index register. We do this so that before returning to the main program (at RESTORE), we can put them back. Since the interrupt could come along any time, we might be executing any part of MAIN. Some part of MAIN surely uses the accumulator and more than likely the index register as well. If we didn't make sure that the interrupt routine returned with the values in A and X as they were upon entry, Murphy's law would insist that the interrupt would strike at just the wrong time, and the main routine would either crash or continue with erroneous values. Actually, we don't change the value in X in HANDLER, but it is good practice to save all the registers anyway in case some later programmers modify HANDLER in such a way that it does use X. They won't have to remember to preserve X. We have made the program safe.

After saving the registers, HANDLER adds one to the count and tests to see if a gross has gone by. If not, we delay to debounce the switch, wait for the switch (and by implication for IRQ also since they are tied together) to go back to one; and if required, debounce this also. The reason we wait for IRQ to go back to one will become clear in a moment. Then we branch to RESTORE. If a gross of widgets has gone by, we ring the bell, stop the line, and wait for the packer to respond. In the next section we will do this by interrupt also, but right now life is complicated enough without that.

When the packer has responded—or right away if less than a gross is in the box—we enter RESTORE, where we reload A and X and execute an RTI (return from interrupt), which takes the top of the stack (which contains $\beta + 1$), puts it into the PC, and then clears the I-bit to zero. Since the PC now contains $\beta + 1$, that is where the next instruction is taken from. This is back in the main program and, in fact, is the next instruction in MAIN that should be executed since we finished up the instruction in β before transferring to the handler. Furthermore, all the registers (A and X) are just the way β finished with them, so we can resume MAIN just as if the interrupt never occurred. If your computer has condition codes, they are usually kept in the PSW, and if that is saved automatically upon interrupt, it will be restored automatically by the RTI instruction. If you had to save it—and you must if it isn't done automatically—then you also have to restore it. If nobody saves the condition codes, then subsequent tests in MAIN will come out wrong, because HANDLER is bound to change at least some of the condition codes.

Finally RTI turns off the I-bit. This is why we had to wait in the interrupt routine until the switch and IRQ went back to one. Otherwise, when we returned to MAIN with the I-bit cleared and IRQ equal to zero, the hardware would have thought that *another* interrupt had occurred and would have jumped off to service that, and we would have counted the same widget several times. There are ways around this delay, which we will explore in the next section.

Exercise 1.1

You will get much more out of this book if you do the exercises we suggest or others that you develop for yourselves to utilize and test out the ideas we discuss. If you have gone through *Programming a Microcomputer: 6502* and done even some of the experiments there, you will find these of the same general type. If not, the first one or two may seem formidable to wire up unless you can get somebody to do it for you or you are acquainted with some elementary electronics. But really you need to know very little about electronics, and that we will try to explain as we go along. For starters we are going to assume that your computer has at least one bidirectional I/O port or one input and one output port with a total of at least two input bits and two output bits and an IRQ line such as we have described.

To begin with, we are going to simulate the widget factory we have discussed above on a simple scale. As a main program, we are going to generate a tone on a cheap loudspeaker. That requires continuous attention of the CPU to make the tone so that you will be able to tell first off if the main program is working, and second you will be able to tell when the CPU gets called away to service the interrupt because the tone will stop. In place of the bell, we will employ a light-emitting diode (LED). If you have never put a push button or a light onto your computer, read Chapter 2 so that you will understand something about I/O ports before continuing.

Connect two momentary-contact single-pole, double-throw switches, as shown in Figure 1.7. When the counter switch is not actuated, input line 1 should be at plus 5 volts, and when actuated, it should go to zero volts. When the packer's switch is not actuated, input line 2 should be at 0 volts, and when the switch is actuated, it should go to plus 5 volts.

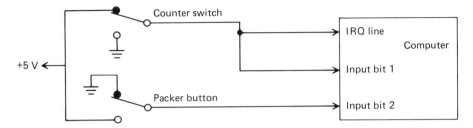

Figure 1.7 *Input connections for Exercise 1.1. Closed circles on switches represent normally closed contacts.*

CHOOSING RESISTORS

In all the circuits of this book the values of the resistors we specify in the diagrams are for guidance only. If we call for 2200-ohm resistor (2200 Ω or 2.2 kΩ), you can substitute one twice as large or half as large, and the circuit will still work. If we call for 2.2K, then you can get away with anything in the range from 1K to 4.7K. So (a) don't make a trip across town just to pick up one resistor if you have anything at all close, and (b) don't waste money on high-precision resistors. The normal tolerance is ±20%, and that's plenty close enough.

Power rating. Resistors come in 1/4 watt, 1/2 watt, 1 watt, and 2 watt varieties. This is an indication of how much power the resistor can dissipate. You will never be wrong using a resistor of high power capability. They just cost a little more. The only place that power capability is important is in the loudspeaker circuit. For that 47 Ω resistor in series with the loudspeaker you should use 1 watt or bigger.

Figure 1.8 shows the output connections. All resistor values are approximate and may be doubled or halved or anywhere in between at your convenience. The transistors shown are NPN type 2N2222. Any NPN transistor capable of handling 100–200 milliamperes may be substituted. The loudspeaker is of approximately 8 ohms impedance, but any cheap ($1.50–$3.00) speaker is acceptable. To test the speaker circuit, disconnect the upper 2200-ohm resistor from the computer and touch it to plus 5 volts and to ground. It should generate "clicks" when you do this. If you do this with the lower 2200-ohm resistor, the LED should go on when you touch plus 5 volts and off when you touch zero. If it does not go on, try reversing the leads of the LED. If you are going to buy cheap LEDs, buy several. They are often bad. Try another if the first one doesn't light up.

Description of the Program

You are to simulate a widget-packing station. At *your* station you put five widgets per box. When no widgets are being detected, a steady hum comes from the

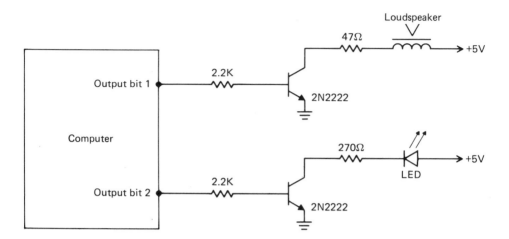

Figure 1.8 *Output connections for Exercise 1.1.*

HOW A LOUDSPEAKER GENERATES SOUNDS

Sound consists of waves of alternating high and low pressure in the air. These pressure waves travel out from the source at about 1000 feet per second. The closer together the peaks of pressure are, and consequently the more pressure waves that strike our ears per second, the higher frequency sound we hear. Middle C on the piano has a frequency of 261.64 cycles per second, or hertz (abbreviated Hz). The C above middle C has a frequency twice that of middle C, and each time we go up one octave on the piano, we double the frequency of the sound waves.

To generate a sound wave, we need to make regions of high pressure followed by regions of low pressure. A loudspeaker does this by moving a diaphragm (the loudspeaker "cone") forward and backward. As the diaphragm moves forward, it squeezes the air in front of it, causing a region of high pressure. As the cone moves backwards, the air rushes in to fill the space left behind by the moving diaphragm and creates a region of low pressure. These pressure waves radiate out from the loudspeaker, and when they reach our ears, we hear a "click."

To make a sound of 250 Hz, we need to move the diaphragm forward 250 times and backward 250 times, all in one second. To make the diaphragm move forward, we pass a current through the "voice coil" of the speaker. To make it move backward, we remove that current, and the diaphragm springs back to its neutral position. A full period from the beginning of one forward movement to the beginning of the next will take 1/250th of a second, or 4 milliseconds (4000 microseconds). So we push the diaphragm forward, wait 2 milliseconds (half a period), pull it back, wait another 2 milliseconds, and do the whole thing again. If we push for 1 millisecond and relax for 1 millisecond, the waves will be only half as far apart, and we will hear a tone of 500 Hz.

loudspeaker, indicating that the main program is functioning. When the widget-counter switch is pressed, a momentary interruption of the tone can be detected as the HANDLER routine notes the passage of another widget. What happens if you hold the widget switch down?

After five widgets have been detected, the LED comes on to tell the packer to change boxes, and the hum ceases. As soon as the packer pushes his switch, the LED goes out and the hum starts up again. Suppose the packer holds his switch down. Does your program still count widgets? What happens when number 5 comes along? What happens if the packer pushes his switch before five widgets come along?

Programming Hints

To generate a hum from the main program, we suggest something like this:

```
MAIN:   LDAIM    128   ⎫
L1:     SUBIM    1     ⎬   Delay loop.
        BPL      L1    ⎭
        LDAIM    1
        OUTPUT   SPEAKER       Set the speaker to 1.
        LDAIM    128   ⎫
L2:     SUBIM    1     ⎬   Delay loop.
        BPL      L2    ⎭
        LDAIM    0
        OUTPUT   SPEAKER       Set speaker to 0.
        JMP      MAIN
```

If the speaker is connected to one bit of an I/O port and the LED to a different bit of the same port, then you have to be more careful about how you turn the speaker on and off, because you don't want to inadvertently change the state of the LED when you change the speaker. Suppose the output port has eight bits numbered 7, 6, . . ., 1, 0, left to right, and the speaker is connected to bit 3, for example.

Keep a copy of what the output port is supposed to look like in a cell called PATTERN. Note that if you can read the pattern stored in the output port, the cell called PATTERN can be the output port itself, but that is not possible on all machines. Then to set the speaker to one, you:

```
LDA      PATTERN      Get the pattern.
IORIM    $04          Or in a 1 at bit 3 (0000 0100).
STA      PATTERN
OUTPUT   OUTPORT
```

and to clear the speaker to zero, you:

```
LDA      PATTERN
ANDIM    $FB          AND the speaker to zero (1111 1011).
STA      PATTERN
OUTPUT   OUTPORT
```

We will use the dollar sign to indicate that the number following it is a hexadecimal (base 16) number.

Using the AND instruction will allow you to pick off single bits from the input port or even a mixed input/output port. To select bit 2 from PORT for test, you can:

```
          INPUT     PORT
          ANDIM     $02          AND with (0000 0010).
```

- Don't forget to tell the hardware where your interrupt processing routine is.
- Turn off the I-bit so that interrupts can take place.
- Save and restore all registers on entry and exit.
- Initialize the stackpointer. The interrupt hardware will use it.
- Initialize the count.

EDGE VERSUS LEVEL

The IRQ line on most computers is what is called a "level detecting" line. To explain what that means, we have to contrast it with an "edge detecting" line. An edge detecting line is one that pays attention only to the change of state on the line. A "leading edge detecting" line is activated only by a change of state from zero to one. A "trailing edge detecting" line is activated only by a change from one to zero. An edge detecting line gives out only one short "yelp" when it detects the appropriate change. If nobody is listening, the event goes unnoticed. A level detecting line is more like a small child that continues to scream until somebody pays attention to it.

Now you can see why the IRQ line has to be of the level detecting type. Suppose the I-bit is set and an edge detecting interrupt line lets out its short "yelp." The yelp is not heard, and the event that caused it is missed. But if the line is a level detector, then whenever the I-bit gets cleared—no matter how long that may take (provided that the level is still maintained and the IRQ line is still "screaming")—the event will be caught and processed. Of course, if the I-bit is set so long that the widget comes under the switch and out again, allowing the IRQ line to go back to one before the I-bit is cleared, that widget will be missed. In the program we have been considering, that won't happen, because we stopped the assembly line until the packer responded, but in other circumstances it might.

Most microcomputers have an additional interrupt line called the NMI (non-maskable interrupt) line. This line is trailing-edge triggered (detects one to zero transitions) and, as its name suggests, pays no attention to the interrupt inhibit bit. When the NMI line gets pulled to ground, no matter what the state of the I-bit, an interrupt is generated, and, in the 6502 at least, control is transferred to the program whose beginning address is stored in an interrupt vector called NMIVEC. This NMI line is normally used as a "manual interrupt"—one generated by the operator of the machine, who wants to get the computer's attention no matter what is going on inside. It would be a shame to have an expensive machine become permanently disabled by turning on the I-bit and then going into a tight loop so that it paid no further attention to anything. Often the NMI line is used as a "power up" interrupt, and when the power is turned on, a signal appears on the NMI line that traps the computer to some known location to begin executing a program stored in ROM (read only memory). In this case, NMIVEC must be a ROM location also, because a RAM location would contain a garbage number at power up time and not the address of the power up routine.

WHAT IS A FLIP-FLOP?

A flip-flop is a device for storing one bit of information. A single flip-flop may store either a 0 or a 1. The output of the flip-flop is called "Q" and is 1 (plus 5 volts) if the flip-flop is storing a 1 and is 0 (0 volts) if the flip-flop holds 0. Often there is another output pin $\overline{Q}$, which is the complement of Q. When Q is 1, $\overline{Q}$ is 0 and vice versa.

Flip-flops come in many varieties, "D" and "JK" being the most common. For our purposes we are concerned only with whether or not they have inputs labeled "P" and "C," or "preset" and "clear." We need these inputs for our circuits.

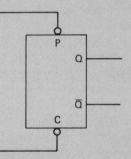

If the diagram of the flip-flop looks like this, it is just exactly what we want. When the line labeled P is forced to 0, the Q will be set to 1 and $\overline{Q}$ cleared to 0. When the line labeled C is forced to 0, then Q will be cleared to 0 and $\overline{Q}$ set to 1. When P and C are not being used to set or clear the flip-flop, they should be left in the logical 1 state (plus 5 volts).

The following flip-flops are all satisfactory for use in our circuits, and without doubt many others exist.

Number and Type	Flip-Flop 1				Flip-Flop 2				Power	
	P_1	C_1	Q_1	$\overline{Q}_1$	P_2	C_2	Q_2	$\overline{Q}_2$	+5 volts	gnd
7470 single JK	13	2	8	6					14	7
7472 single JK	13	2	8	6					14	7
7476 dual JK	2	3	15	14	7	8	11	10	5	13
7479 dual D	4	1	5	6	10	13	9	8	14	7
74109 dual JK	5	1	6	7	11	15	10	9	16	8

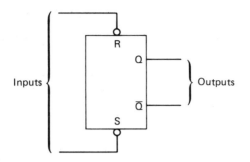

Figure 1.9 *A flip-flop with active low R and S lines.*

CLEARING AN INTERRUPT

In the discussion and exercise above, we connected the counting switch directly to the IRQ line, and consequently the computer had to wait until the widget passed by the switch before it could leave the interrupt routine. But if widgets come down the assembly line, one right on another's heels, the computer might end up spending a large fraction of its time waiting for the switch to clear. There is a way around this, but it will require some external hardware.

A flip-flop is a semiconductor device used to store one bit of information. The type we want to consider here is called an R-S flip-flop. They have two inputs called RESET (R) and SET (S) and two outputs labeled Q and $\overline{Q}$ (read "queue bar"). $\overline{Q}$ is the logical complement of Q. If Q is 1 (plus 5 volts), then $\overline{Q}$ will be 0 (0 volts), and if Q is 0, then $\overline{Q}$ will be 1. (See Figure 1.9.) There are many TTL flip-flops available, of which the 7474 is but one example.

When the RESET line (sometimes called the CLEAR line) is brought to logical 0, then Q goes to 0 and $\overline{Q}$ goes to 1. If R now goes back to 1, this output state will persist. If the SET line (sometimes called the PRESET line) goes to 0, then Q will go to 1 and $\overline{Q}$ will go to 0. This state will be stable and persist until R goes to 0 again.

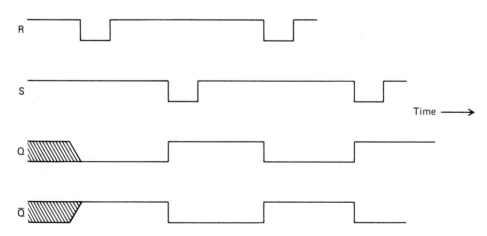

Figure 1.10 *Relationship of the outputs of the flip-flop to pulses on the R and S lines.*

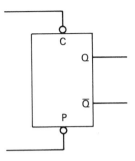

Figure 1.11 *Clear and preset (C and P) are sometimes used in place of reset and set (R and S).*

(Note that if both R and S are 0 at the same time, the output is indeterminate. Some flip-flops will put both Q and $\overline{Q}$ to 0. Others may not.) So the flip-flop "remembers" whether R or S was 0 most recently. (See Figure 1.10.)

When you select a flip-flop for use, look carefully at its circuit diagram. If there are small circles next to its R and S (or C and P) inputs, as in Figure 1.11, then those lines are "active low," and Q will be set to 1 when P goes to 0 and reset to 0 when C goes to 0.

DEBOUNCING A SWITCH

At this point we know enough to debounce a switch electronically. Figure 1.12 shows the technique. Remember that electronic circuits such as flip-flops need electrical power in order to operate. TTL circuits require a supply of approximately 5 volts DC. Power connections are never shown on circuit diagrams. The positive side of the power supply ($+5$) is connected to the pin on the chip labeled V_{CC}, and the negative side of the supply (0) to the pin labeled GND. All circuits on a chip share the same power supply. It is considered good practice to connect a small ceramic disc capacitor between the V_{CC} and GND pins of each and every chip—as near to the chip as possible. TTL circuits draw a lot of current for a short period when changing state, and these capacitors will supply that, thus keeping "spikes" from appearing on the power lines and possibly causing other circuits to malfunction. Usual practice calls for .05 to .5 microfarads capable of withstanding 10 to 15 volts.

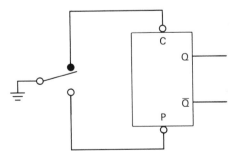

Figure 1.12 *Debouncing a switch using active low clear and preset inputs to a flip-flop.*

A regulated 5-volt DC supply capable of producing one or two amperes (amps) of current would be a worthwhile investment. You can purchase or build one for under $30. If you are not going to use such a supply very often, then three flashlight batteries (D cells) in series will do. When new and not heavily loaded, they produce 1.5 volts apiece, and 4.5 volts is just within tolerance for a TTL supply. Better than that would be a pack of four 1.2 volt Nicad rechargeable cells, such as are used for radio control receivers. This will supply 5 volts and has a low internal impedance, so you can load it down quite a bit. Don't forget to recharge the pack once in a while. Disconnect the batteries from your TTL circuitry while recharging them. Often your computer will have a 5-volt supply built into it, and you can "steal" a bit of power from that supply. Do not attempt to drive more than three or four TTL chips this way unless you know there is plenty of power available above and beyond what the computer itself needs.

Have you succeeded in debouncing your switch? The circuit of Figure 1.12 *assumes* that the switch is so constructed that the center arm (transfer contact) doesn't bounce so hard that it makes contact with both output terminals. It should leave the output terminal it is in contact with and then make intermittent contact with the other terminal but never come back to contact the first terminal until the switch is operated in the other direction. If this assumption is valid (and it is for most switches), then the output of the flip-flop should be a clean transition from 0 to 5 V (or 5 V to 0) with no bounce at all. The best way to determine if this is the case is to use an oscilloscope. If you don't have a scope handy, then you can use your computer as a test instrument. Connect the output (either Q or $\overline{Q}$) of the flip-flop to an input bit of the computer. (You must make sure that the ground of your computer—usually the case is grounded—and the ground of your power supply are connected together.)

CAUTION: Voltages in excess of 5 volts connected to input pins may damage your computer.

Program the computer to look for a change in input and when it finds one to make a record of any changes that occur over the next couple of milliseconds. (See *Programming a Microcomputer: 6502* for details.) Try this with a debounced switch and with a switch that is not debounced.

A CLEARABLE INTERRUPT

Now that we have a debounced switch, we can approach the problem we set out to solve of having an interrupt that we can clear. Figure 1.13 shows the circuit we want to talk about. It is constructed using a 7474, but any dual flip-flop with unclocked reset/set inputs will do. The left-hand flip-flop is used to debounce the switch. When the switch is not operated (in the normally closed position), the clear input will be pulled to ground, and so Q will equal 0 and $\overline{Q}$ will equal 1. When the switch is operated, Q will go to 1 and $\overline{Q}$ to 0. The .001 microfarad capacitor that connects pin 6 to pin 10 is there to differentiate this change. That means that when $\overline{Q}$ goes to 0, it passes a short negative pulse, and when $\overline{Q}$ goes to 1, it passes a

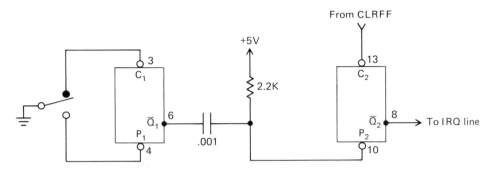

Figure 1.13 *A clearable interrupt using a dual flip-flop. Pin numbers shown are for a 7474.*

short positive pulse. The positive pulses (when they occur) have no effect on the second flip-flop, but the negative pulses force the P input of the second flip-flop to ground momentarily. This momentary 0 potential on P_2 is enough to preset the second flip-flop, setting Q_2 to 1 and $\overline{Q}_2$ to 0. When $\overline{Q}_2$ goes to 0, it pulls down the IRQ line, which interrupts the computer.

At this point the computer transfers control to the interrupt-handling routine. This routine has to be modified to clear the second flip-flop so that we can go back to the main routine. The switch is going to have no further effect on the second flip-flop until it is released and then operated again. Assume that the line CLRFF is connected to bit 0 of an output port. Then after we save registers, the next thing to do in the interrupt handler is to bring CLRFF to 0 for a moment (one microsecond or less will do) and then return it to logical 1 (plus 5 volts). We can do this as follows:

```
LDAIM      0
OUTPUT     CLRFF
LDAIM      1
OUTPUT     CLRFF
```

We must remember to leave CLRFF at logical 1 (except when we are actively clearing the flip-flop), because otherwise a value of 0 on C_2 will prevent $\overline{Q}_2$ from going to 0.

Exercise 1.2

With the above circuit we no longer have to wait until the widget has passed the switch before going back to the main program. Construct the above circuit and modify your program from Exercise 1.1 so that when you operate the widget counting switch, there may be a click in the sound output by the speaker, but no matter how long you hold down the widget switch, there is only this click, and then the hum continues. When the box is full, the hum will disappear until the packer pushes his button, of course. We will take care of *that* in the next section. Note that for *this* exercise you don't need to be able to test the value of the signal put on the IRQ line.

TWO INTERRUPTS

In the previous sections we have been concerned with only one interrupting condition. Now we are going to study how you can get a computer to tell which of two conditions caused the interrupt. What we want to do is to count widgets with a switch, as we did in Exercise 1.2, and further to allow the computer to go back to the main program and execute that while waiting for the packer to respond. We will interrupt the main routine whenever we detect a widget, and we will also inter-

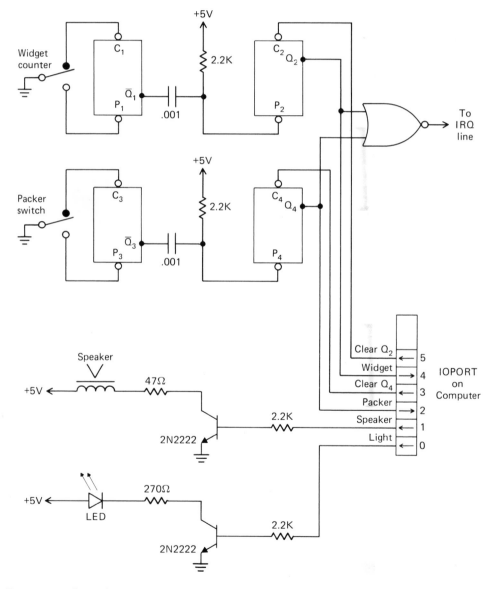

Figure 1.14 *Setup for two interrupts.*

rupt it whenever the packer pushes his button, but since different actions are to be carried out in the two cases, we will have to be able to tell who caused the interrupt. For the sake of specificity, we are going to assume in our discussion that we have a bidirectional I/O port called IOPORT.

Figure 1.14 shows the circuit for this two-interrupt situation. The two switches are debounced as before, but this time we take the Q outputs of flip-flops 2 and 4 (which go to 1 when the switches are actuated) and present them to the inputs of a NOR circuit. A NOR gives an output of 1 if neither of its inputs is 1, so when either Q_2 or Q_4 goes to 1, this causes the output of the NOR (and hence the IRQ line) to go to 0, interrupting the computer.

Lines from Q_2 and Q_4 also go to bits 4 and 2 of IOPORT so that with a little judicious programming we will be able to test to see which one of them caused the interrupt. Bits 5 and 3 of IOPORT are output bits that should normally have 1's on them. When we wish to clear the interrupt from the widget counter, we put a 0 on bit 5. Bit 0 of IOPORT controls the LED, and a logical 1 there will cause the light to go on. Care should be taken to change only one of these bits at a time—not because the circuit will be damaged but for programming reasons.

Figure 1.15 shows a flow diagram of the interrupt program. We enter at the top whenever an interrupt occurs and immediately save all machine registers. Next

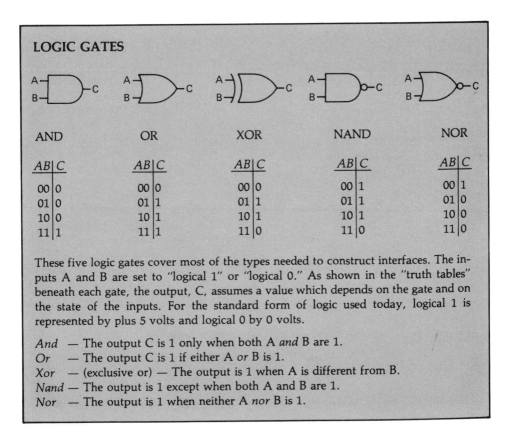

LOGIC GATES

AND	OR	XOR	NAND	NOR
$AB\|C$	$AB\|C$	$AB\|C$	$AB\|C$	$AB\|C$
00 0	00 0	00 0	00 1	00 1
01 0	01 1	01 1	01 1	01 0
10 0	10 1	10 1	10 1	10 0
11 1	11 1	11 0	11 0	11 0

These five logic gates cover most of the types needed to construct interfaces. The inputs A and B are set to "logical 1" or "logical 0." As shown in the "truth tables" beneath each gate, the output, C, assumes a value which depends on the gate and on the state of the inputs. For the standard form of logic used today, logical 1 is represented by plus 5 volts and logical 0 by 0 volts.

And — The output C is 1 only when both A *and* B are 1.
Or — The output C is 1 if either A *or* B is 1.
Xor — (exclusive or) — The output is 1 when A is different from B.
Nand — The output is 1 except when both A and B are 1.
Nor — The output is 1 when neither A *nor* B is 1.

LOGIC CHIPS

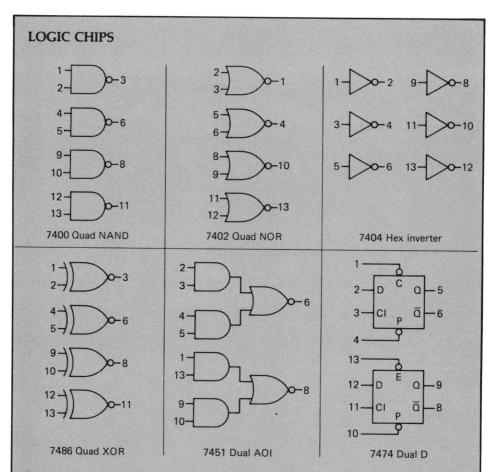

7400 Quad NAND   7402 Quad NOR   7404 Hex inverter

7486 Quad XOR   7451 Dual AOI   7474 Dual D

Several hundred different chips are available in the logic family known as TTL— transistor transistor logic. Several subfamilies are available. For example, a 7400 is a standard hex inverter, a 74L00 is a low-power version of the 7400. A 74S00 is a Schottky version offering high speed, and the 74LS00 is a low-power, high-speed version. For our purposes the different versions are all equally suitable. Circuit diagrams such as the above show the chips looking down on the top with the pins pointing away from the viewer. There is a dot next to pin 1 or else a notch on the end of the chip where pin 1 is located.

We strongly recommend the use of sockets when building circuits. Remember that when you are connecting wires to the sockets, you will be looking up at the chips from underneath. Either solder connections or wire wrap sockets can be used, depending on your preference. You can solder to wire wrap sockets with no trouble, but the reverse is certainly not true.

Power must be supplied to each chip. For all those shown above, +5 volts is connected to pin 14, and pin 7 is connected to ground.

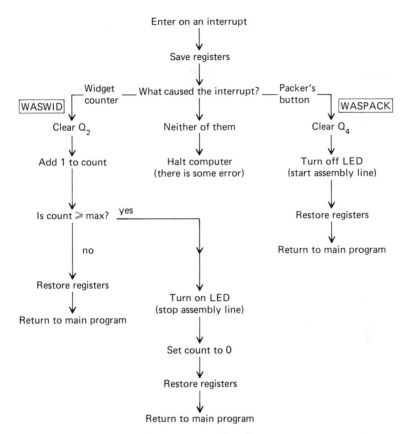

Figure 1.15 *A flow diagram of the program to handle two interrupts.*

we try to determine what caused the interrupt. This can be done with code similar to the following:

```
INPUT     IOPORT
ANDIM     $10          (Mask pattern 0001 0000.)
BNA       WASWID       Bit 4 set means widget switch.
INPUT     IOPORT
ANDIM     $04          (Mask pattern 0000 0100.)
BNA       WASPACK      Nonzero bit 2 means packer button.
HLT                    Stop the computer.
```

If neither switch was operated and we got an interrupt, we have trouble somewhere. It is redundant but very wise to write programs this way rather than just to assume that if it isn't the widget switch, it *must* be the packer button. It usually will be, but what, heaven forfend, if there is a programming error someplace?

Let us assume it was the widget switch. The first thing to do in this case is to clear Q_2 so that when we return to the main program, Q_2 is not still calling for an interrupt. We do this in such a way that we don't change the output on either bit 2 or bit 0 when we clear Q_2:

LDA	PATTERN	Pattern is 110 if the LED is off and 111 if the LED is on.
ANDIM	$FD	Clear bit 1 (1111 1101).
OUTPUT	IOPORT	Put it out, resetting Q_2.
LDA	PATTERN	
OUTPUT	IOPORT	Bring bit 1 back to 1.

Now, it is obvious why we don't want to change output bit 0 and hence the state of the LED, but why shouldn't we clear both interrupt flip-flops at the same time? The reason is that both interrupts might occur at very nearly the same time. Suppose that just as the Nth widget comes under the switch, an alert packer pushes his button, saying that he is changing the box. There are three possibilities to worry about: Q_4 gets set to 1 while we are saving registers and deciding which interrupt occurred; Q_4 gets set to 1 after we have cleared Q_2 but before returning to the main program; or Q_4 doesn't get set until we return to the main program.

In the third case, when Q_4 comes along after we have finished processing Q_2, there is no problem. We have two successive independent interrupts with no interaction between them. In case 2, when Q_4 comes along after we have cleared Q_2, the IRQ line will be pulled to 0 again, but since the first interrupt set the I-bit to 1, Q_4 will cause no effect until after WASWID executes its RTI, clearing the I-bit, and tries to return to the main program. As soon as the I-bit is cleared with IRQ at 0, an interrupt occurs—this new one caused by Q_4.

In the first case, where Q_4 goes to 1 before Q_2 is cleared, we must be careful to clear Q_2 without disturbing Q_4, because we do want to honor the Q_4 interrupt and not miss it.

Take note of the fact that if both interrupts occur at the same time, we will always service Q_2 before we service Q_4. That is because we test for Q_2 first. We could, of course, reverse the order of the tests if we felt that Q_4 was more important than Q_2. We will return to the problem of which interrupt to process first in Chapter 3, but meanwhile we are going to explore I/O in some detail in Chapter 2.

Exercise 1.3

Using the circuit of Figure 1.14, reprogram Exercise 1.2 so that the CPU does not wait for either switch. Now the hum you generate should never stop. There may be slight "clicks" when a button is pushed and an output is delayed, but other than that it should be continuous. Every fifth push of the widget counter should cause the LED to come on and stay on until the packer's button is pushed.

2 Ports

This chapter is concerned with the units known as "ports," which allow us to connect a CPU to a peripheral device. The closest thing to a port that comes to mind from real life is a bilingual interpreter who can tell A in English what B just said in French—and vice versa. A port is intended to match the electrical characteristics of the CPU with those of the peripheral.

We will consider first how peripheral devices can communicate with the central processing unit (CPU) via memory mapping or via I/O instructions. Then we will look at three typical devices: an eight-bit parallel port, a one-bit asynchronous receiver/transmitter, and a time/event counter. Finally we will look at one real peripheral interface unit.

REACHING THE DEVICE

Figure 2.1 shows two idealized microcomputers, one with separate buses for memory and I/O and the other with memory and I/O devices on the same bus. In the first there are completely separate paths for memory and I/O while in the second I/O devices are treated as specialized cells of regular memory. In the first scheme the computer must have two sets of instructions, one for referencing memory, such as Load accumulator or Add to accumulator, and a second set to perform I/O, such as Read from device N or Write to device N. In the second scheme you say "Load accumulator from X," and if X happens to be a memory cell, you get the contents of cell X, but if X happens to be the name of an I/O device, you get the next character from that device.

The advantage of the first scheme is that I/O devices don't take up memory address space. On the other hand, the input/output instructions do use up some of the op-code patterns that might have been used for something else. In memory-mapped I/O you get the full power of the CPU's instruction set applied to input and output. For instance, one can "add" from a device or "increment" the number being output.

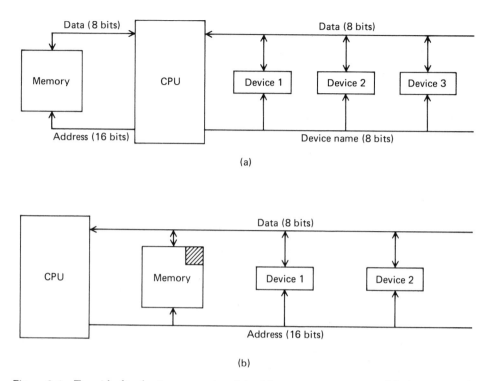

Figure 2.1 *Two idealized microcomputers (a) with separate memory and I/O access paths, similar to the Z-80, and (b) with "memory-mapped" I/O, similar to the 6502.*

The Z-80 and 8080 are examples of machines with I/O instructions, and the 6502 and 6800 are examples of machines using memory-mapped I/O.

The more "modern" approach is the one called "memory mapping." It *can* be employed by any computer and *must* be employed by those without separate I/O instructions. In this scheme I/O devices are assigned addresses in main memory. Sometimes one takes a particular block of storage addresses, say, cells F000 thru FFFF, and reserves them for I/O. Other times the devices can be scattered around address space, using memory-mapped I/O at will. One can easily give a device "control registers" that also have memory addresses and that the CPU can load or sample, using standard instructions.

RECOGNIZING YOUR NAME

Be you I/O device or memory cell, you must hold up your hand and shout "Here" when your name is called. An address is broadcast on the address lines by the CPU, and each device watches those lines, looking for its own address.

When the CPU wants to read from a given memory location, it does three things:

1.   The CPU places the name of the desired location on the address lines.

2. The CPU sets the READ/WRITE line to READ.

3. The CPU asserts the "address valid" line, telling the memory and devices that they can now look at the address lines without fear that the lines are in the process of changing.

At the memory and devices, the address is compared with the name of the device by inverting the address lines that correspond to zeros in the name (so they will be ones) and looking for all ones at the input to the AND gate that is the "recognizer." The device shown in Figure 2.2 will respond to the name 10110011 and no other. An 8-bit recognizer is sufficient for selecting one of 256 possible I/O devices. Two such recognizers, one hooked up to address lines A0–A7 and the other to address lines A8–A15 will select one of 2^{16} possible addresses when *both* their outputs are logical one.

When a manufacturer makes an I/O card, he does not know where you may want to put it in either I/O device space or main memory address space. Consequently, the usual thing to do is to make the address the card responds to selectable by the user. To do this the manufacturer often includes a set of switches that allow the user to change the "name" the card answers to. These are usually normally open switches connected to the inputs of exclusive or gates (see Figure 2.3).

When a switch is open, the input to the associated XOR is pulled up to a logical 1 (plus 5 volts) by the 2.2K resistor. When the switch is closed, the input is held at logical 0 (ground). The XOR generates a logical 1 if its two inputs differ, and the AND outputs a 1 if all its inputs are 1. So by opening or closing the switches, one can vary the address the circuit will respond to.

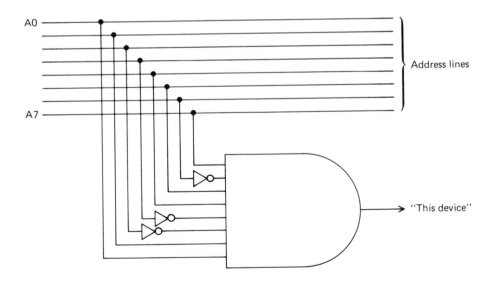

Figure 2.2 *A recognizer for "10110011."*

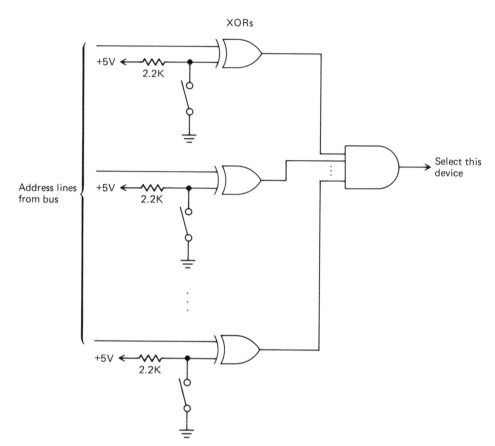

Figure 2.3 *Realization of a changeable device selector.*

INPUT OUTPUT PORT

Let us design a very simple output port and an even simpler input port for a computer. Figure 2.4 shows one bit of each. When control line C_1 is raised to logical one, the value on the input line is presented to the data bus line. When C_1 is zero, the input gate allows the data bus line to "float" and does not try to force it to either zero or one. This is called a "tri-state" gate, and we can connect a number of them in parallel as long as only one is turned on at a time. When C_2 is raised to one, the edge-triggered D-type flip-flop makes a copy of what is on the data bus line and will "remember it" until C_2 goes to one again. Meanwhile, the value stored in the flip-flop is output on the "output" line. We can activate C_1 whenever the right address appears together with a read (or input) signal, and we can activate C_2 when the proper address coincides with a write (or output) signal.

Often we wish to make a port that can be either input or output, depending on how we set some switch. This is usually done on a "per bit" basis, and we have a second storage register called a "direction" register, which specifies (for every bit of

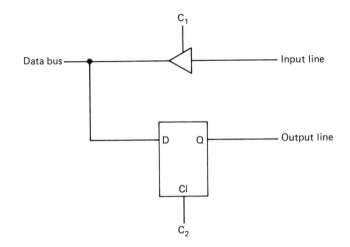

Figure 2.4 *A simple input and output circuit for one bit. The input is controlled by C_1 turning on or off a gated amplifier. The output comes from a D-type flip-flop. When the clock input goes to 1, the D line is sampled and held until the next clock signal.*

the data register) whether it will be an input or an output bit. Often a direction register has a separate address or name distinct from that of the data register it controls. Sometimes these addresses are right next to each other, but there are no physical reasons requiring this.

Figure 2.5 shows a data register and a direction register, each with its own recognizer. The data register or the direction register or neither may be connected to the CPU's data bus, depending on what address is on the address bus.

ONE-SHOT TIMER

Figure 2.6 shows a so-called one-shot timer. These may be of any length, but 8 and 16 bits are the usual numbers. A 16-bit timer on an 8-bit machine has separate addresses for the upper half of the counter and the lower half of the counter. Typically, a number is loaded into the counter and it starts running, subtracting one from that number on every tick of the clock. When the number in the counter reaches zero, an interrupt flag is raised, and the main program is interrupted if the system is enabled. This interrupt flag may then be cleared by reading or writing the lower or the upper half. During the count down to zero, the program may look at the number of microseconds remaining by reading from the upper and lower. Since this count is continually changing, some caution is urged upon the person who desires to do this.

Repeater

A repeater (see Figure 2.7) is like a one-shot, except that it has a 16-bit buffer in addition to the 16-bit count register. Each of the four 8-bit bytes (buffer upper and

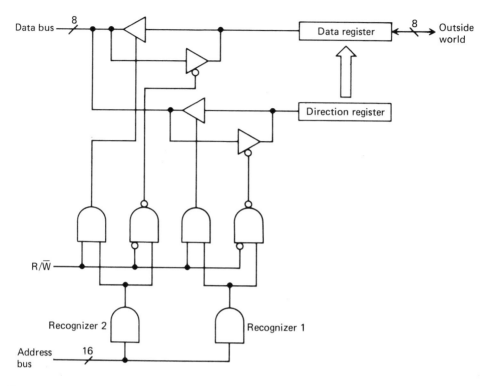

Figure 2.5 *A bidirectional port with its direction register. The slash and a number on a line indicate that the line is replicated that number of times.*

lower and counter upper and lower) will have its own address in an 8-bit machine. Loading the upper half of the buffer causes the entire contents of the buffer to be transferred to the counter and the counter to begin to count down. When the count reaches zero, the interrupt flag is set, and the contents of the buffer are reloaded into the counter, and the count down is begun again. Reading the counter-lower will clear the interrupt flag as before. Repeaters are extremely useful when a steady stream of evenly spaced pulses or interrupts is desired. These can be used directly as a clock or to drive a waveform generator or a UART (see next section).

Event Counter

An event counter (see Figure 2.8) looks just like a one-shot, except that instead of a clock being connected to the counter, an external line is provided. Each time that line goes from zero to one we subtract one from the number stored in the counter. By loading a number into the counter, we can cause it to generate an interrupt after N events have occurred, or if we start off with FFFF in the counter, we can tell how many events (modulo 2^{16}) have occurred by taking the one's complement of the number now in the counter.

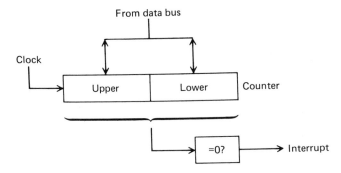

Figure 2.6 *A one-shot timer.*

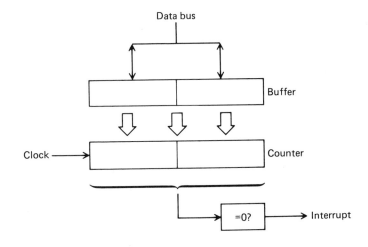

Figure 2.7 *A repeating counter.*

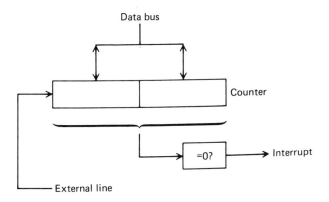

Figure 2.8 *An event counter.*

Since all three of these options (one-shot, repeater, and counter) are basically very similar, they are often sold as a single timer chip with an additional register called the control register provided to select one of the three options and to handle interrupt flag and mask.

Exercise 2.1

Given a one-shot, make it behave like a repeating counter by appropriate software.

SERIAL PORTS

Some microprocessors provide two lines direct from the outside world to the CPU. One line the CPU can test for zero or one. The other line is connected to a one-bit register the CPU can load. The value the CPU puts in that register appears on the outside line ready and able to influence the universe. Using those two lines and proper programming, you can replace everything we are going to discuss in this section. There are two major reasons for using serial as opposed to parallel ports. The first is to conserve pins on a computer chip. Pins (connections with the outside world) are a precious commodity in current chip design. The other reason is to conserve copper wire. Given a slow peripheral with moving parts like a teletypewriter, one pair of wires in bit serial operation is fast enough to keep up with the peripheral. For the present we will concentrate on the Universal Asynchronous Receiver and Transmitter (UART) chip.

Figure 2.9 shows in outline form a typical UART.

Action begins when an 8-bit character is written into buffer TA by the CPU. If the transmitter side of the UART is idle, this character is copied into buffer TB, where it is disassembled into 8 serial bits preceded by a single start bit and followed by one or two stop bits (determined by the control register). This packet of 10 or 11 bits is sent out on the output line, one at a time, at a rate determined by the clock.

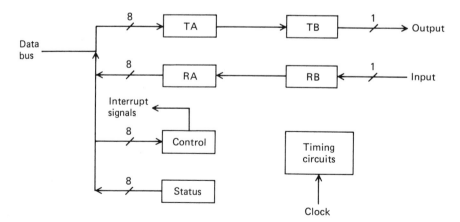

Figure 2.9 *A typical UART.*

When the last bit has been sent, an interrupt flag is usually raised, and the character from TA is copied over to TB, clearing a flip-flop called "TA full" to zero. The CPU then reloads TA, which clears the "transmitter" interrupt flag and sets TA full to 1. If, when the last bit is sent from TB, TA full is zero, then TA is judged to be empty (the CPU hasn't refilled it), and the transmitter falls idle. By coupling a UART with a repeating counter, one can adjust the speed of transmission (and reception) to match that of almost any peripheral device desired from 10 characters per second (110 bits/sec—11 bits per character) to 120 characters per second (1200 bits per second—10 bits per character) or even higher.

The UART may also function as a receiver. When a start bit comes along on the input line, the receiver gets itself ready to receive 8 information bits, which it copies, one by one, into RB. When the first stop bit comes in, the character in RB is copied into RA, and the receiver interrupt flag is raised. The CPU responds by reading RA, which clears the receiver interrupt flag.

At any time the CPU can read the status register, which will tell it good things like which interrupt flag is up and whether a faulty character was received. The control register will allow the programmer to mask out either, both, or neither of the interrupts, and to perform certain other functions peculiar to the actual chip you have purchased.

Exercise 2.2

Assume your computer has a serial output bit. Assume you have a typewriter that can accept 30 characters per second, one start bit ($=0$), eight information bits, and one stop bit ($=1$) per character. Write a subroutine that will take 8-bit characters presented in the accumulator and output these characters to the teletype.

PERIPHERAL INTERFACE ADAPTERS—PIAs

One of the great advantages of recent advances in semiconductor technology is the fact that we can now get quite complex devices on a single chip. The PIA is a good example of this. There are a number of versions of PIAs around. We will concentrate on the logically interchangeable versions made by Motorola and M.O.S. Technology called the 6820 and the 6520.

Such a device is shown in Figure 2.10. It consists of six registers divided into two groups of three. Each of the two sides, A and B, has a control register, a direction register and an I/O port. As can be seen from the figure, only four addresses are assigned to the six registers, so the port and direction registers of each side have to share an address. Bit 2 of the respective control register is used to select which of the pair is being talked to at any given time. If bit 2 of control register CA is 0, then address 00 refers to direction register DA. If that bit is one, address 00 refers to the data register RA. Figure 2.11 shows the addressing in detail. The bits of the direction registers determine whether the corresponding bits of the corresponding port are input or output. If bit i of DA is 1 (which looks like an "I" which stands for input) then bit i of RA is an *output* bit. If bit i of DA is 0 (which looks like an "oh" for

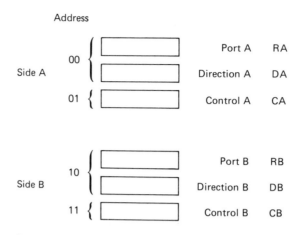

Figure 2.10 *General picture of a PIA.*

output), then bit i of RA is input. That's right, it's backwards. Sorry about that. Actually there is a reason for this choice. When you turn a computer on, the values of many of its internal bits are randomly one or zero. An output port with random numbers in it might conceivably damage some peripheral device. An input port cannot. The "reset" pulse of many microcomputers is used to "clear" all sorts of bits (including direction registers) to zero. To protect peripherals, "zeros" are made to be input.

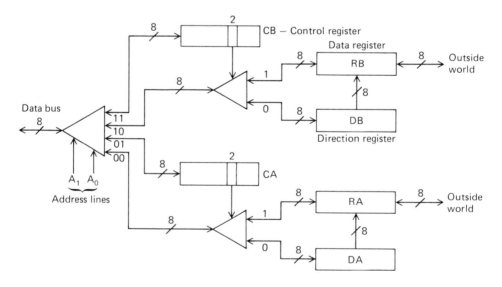

Figure 2.11 *Details of the addressing of a 6520 PIA. The notation /8 indicates that there are eight lines, one for each bit. The triangles represent path selectors, which connect one of the sets of lines on the flat side of a triangle to the set of lines at its apex. Which connections are made is determined by the lines going into the sloping sides.*

So to output an 8-bit pattern on port A, you have to do the following. Assuming F000 is the base address assigned to this PIA:

1.	LDAIM	$00	Put all zeros in accumulator.
2.	STA	$F001	Store it in CA.

This gets the PIA so we can address the direction register.

3.	LDAIM	$FF	Get all ones in the AC.
4.	STA	F000	Store it in the direction register, making the port be output.
5.	LDAIM	$04	Get the pattern 000 0100.
6.	STA	F001	Store it in CA, selecting the port instead of the direction register.
7.	LDA	pattern	Get the pattern.
8.	STA	$F000	Store it in the port.

Of course, we don't have to repeat steps 1–6 every time if we want to output a string of patterns but only when we set up at power-on time or when we want to turn the port around from input to output, or vice versa.

To do the same thing to port B, we would have to write:

1.	LDAIM	$00
2.	STA	$F003
3.	LDAIM	$FF
4.	STA	$F002
5.	LDAIM	$04
6.	STA	$F003
7.	LDA	pattern
8.	STA	$F002

To make the port be input, we change the FF of step 3 to 00, and then we had better change steps 7 and 8 to:

LDA	$F002	Get the input from port B.
STA	someplace	Put it away.

PIA INTERRUPT LINES

In addition to the things talked about already, each side of a PIA has three additional lines connected to it which are used in a fairly complicated fashion for interrupts and handshaking with such things as printers and tape readers and the like. Consider first the interrupts. Bits 6 and 7 of each of the control registers (A and B) are called "flag bits" and can be connected to generate interrupts of the CPU whenever they go to logical one.

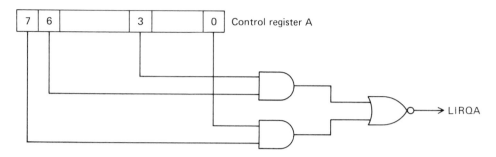

Figure 2.12 *Interrupt-control circuits built into the A side of a 6520 PIA.*

The mechanism is best explained by reference to Figure 2.12. This shows the circuits on the A side of the PIA. Identical circuits exist on the B side connecting CB to LIRQB.

Bits 3 and 0 of the control register are used as "masks" to connect or inhibit the connection of flags 6 and 7 to the "local interrupt request" (LIRQ). If bit 3 is 0, then flag 6 is disconnected. If bit 3 is 1, then flag 6 is connected. Similarly, bit 0 is "ANDED" with flag 7. If one of the flags is connected (its mask is 1) and the flag in turn is 1, then the local interrupt request line is pulled down to logical zero. Since the IRQ input to the 6502 and the 6800 are "active low" (that is, are considered to be "true" when logical zero is applied to them), if we connect LIRQA to the IRQ input to the CPU, we will get an interrupt.

So we can interrupt the CPU (if we want to) by unmasking either bit 6 or 7 of the control register, and whenever that bit goes to one, we have an interrupt. All we need to know now is how to make bits 6 or 7 go to one and how to make them go back to zero again. The latter is easy. Anytime the CPU reads or writes in the input/output register (RA or RB) associated with the control register, both flags are cleared to zero. Reading the control register or the direction register won't do it. Just the data register.

The designers of the 6502 CPUs provided a convenient feature for us. The instruction "bit test" (BIT) can be used to copy the flags of a control register into the condition codes of the processor status word, so they can be tested easily. BIT will

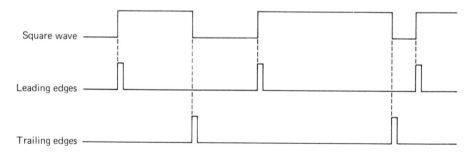

Figure 2.13 *A square wave and markers signaling the zero-to-one transition (leading edges) and one-to-zero transition (trailing edges).*

copy bit 7 of the memory word into condition code N as you would expect, but it also copies bit 6 of the memory word into the overflow bit V, so you can do a "branch on overflow" to check that bit.

Now how do we get the flags to go to 1? This is where the other two lines on each side of the PIA come in. To explain this, we first need to review the concept of an "edge detector." These come in two varieties: leading edge detectors (abbreviated LEDD) and trailing edge detectors (abbreviated TEDD). Consider the square wave shown in Figure 2.13. When it goes from zero to one, this is called the "leading edge" of the wave. When it goes back down from one to zero, this is called the "trailing edge."

C_1 (bit 1 of the control register) is used to determine whether C_7 will be set by a leading edge of I_1 or a trailing edge of I_1. $C_1 = 1$ means leading edge and $C_1 = 0$ means trailing edge (see Figure 2.14).

The control of C_6 is more complicated. As shown in Figure 2.14, there are three bits used to control the interaction of C_6 and I_2. If $C_5 = 0$, then C_4C_3 control C_6 from I_2, just as C_1C_0 control C_7 from I_1.

If, however, $C_5 = 1$, then C_6 is not set under any condition, and I_2 becomes an output bit. If the control bits ($C_5C_4C_3$) are 100, then I_2 does whatever C_7 does. An external event that is sampled by I_1 and sets C_7 will also set I_2. When C_7 is cleared (by reading or writing the RA or RB register), then I_2 will tell the outside world about it. We will talk more about this later when we consider "handshaking." Con-

---

$C_1\ C_0$

0 0	C_7 is set when I_1 goes to 0. Does not cause an interrupt.
0 1	C_7 is set when I_1 goes to 0. Does pull LIRQ to zero for interrupt.
1 0	C_7 is set when I_1 goes to 1. Does not cause an interrupt.
1 1	C_7 is set when I_1 goes to 1. Does pull LIRQ to zero for interrupt.

$C_5\ C_4\ C_3$

0 0 0	C_6 is set when I_2 goes to 0. Does not cause an interrupt.
0 0 1	C_6 is set when I_2 goes to 0. Does pull LIRQ to zero for interrupt.
0 1 0	C_6 is set when I_2 goes to 1. Does not cause an interrupt.
0 1 1	C_6 is set when I_2 goes to 1. Does pull LIRQ to zero for interrupt.
1 0 0	I_2 follows C_7—used for handshaking.
1 0 1	I_2 gives pulse on read (type A) or write (type B) of R register.
1 1 0	$I_2 = 0$.
1 1 1	$I_2 = 1$.

C_2 or R/D

0	Even address to port goes to direction register D.
1	Even address to port goes to I/O register R.

Figure 2.14 *Summary of control register.*

trol bits equal to 101 cause another form of handshaking to take place. In this mode I_2 gives a short (1 microsecond) pulse when the R register is referenced. Here we find the major logical difference between type A and type B ports. Type A will give this pulse when the CPU *reads* R (consumes the data in the I/O port), whereas type B gives this pulse when the CPU *writes* R (produces new output data).

Finally, if $C_5C_4 = 11$, then I_2 will follow C_3 and do whatever it does.

Exercise 2.3

This is a paper exercise, but you can turn it into a real one if you have a PIA or a PIA-like device connected to your computer. If you do not already own such a device, it is probably not worthwhile to buy one just for this exercise, although you will surely get more from actually programming the device than from talking about programming it, and the device might be useful in its own right.

The exercise is to redo Exercise 1.3, using a PIA as an interface between the two buttons and the computer. As in Figure 2.15, connect two debounced switches to the interrupt lines I_{1A} and I_{1B}, and connect local interrupt request lines A and B (LIRQA and LIRQB) together to the IRQ pin of the computer. Assume that the PIA is memory-mapped at address ADDPIA. Rewrite Exercise 1.3. Set up the IRQVEC; set up the control registers for interrupt on pressing the buttons. Remember to save registers and to clear the interrupt flags in the control registers.

Exercise 2.4

Assume that the second button is connected to I_{2A} instead of I_{1B}. What changes do you have to make to the above?

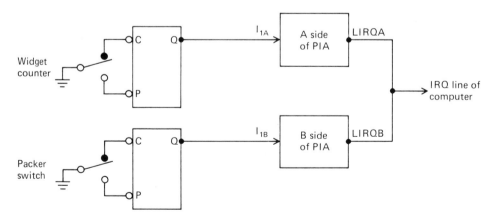

Figure 2.15 *The circuit connections for Exercise 2.3.*

3 Multiple Interrupts

In Chapter 1 we discussed simple interrupts and got as far as a system with two interrupts. In this chapter we are going to discuss what happens if you want to let an interrupt routine get interrupted by another event.

NESTING INTERRUPTS

Suppose we have a situation in which we want one computer to take care of three different processes. Let's call them A, B, and C. Process A is a process that has relatively low importance, but it is one that can utilize the computer any time the machine is available. Process B is one that doesn't require full time attention of a computer but that needs occasional service at moderate priority. For example, process B might entail printing out characters on a typewriter. We want to keep the typewriter busy so we can get our report typed out, but this will require only a few microseconds every 30th of a second. Process C is a relatively rarely invoked process, but when an event occurs that requires the services of process C, we had better drop everything else and tend to C at once.

To put this in a context familiar to most of us, let process A represent writing a book—something that is an infinite sink for time. Process B is a student knocking on your office door with a question about tomorrow's homework, and process C is a phone call from the dean. You stop doing A to take care of either B or C. If you are doing B when C comes along, you stop doing B long enough to take care of C, then go back to finish B, and when that's finished, you go back to process A. Figure 3.1 displays an abstract diagram of the situation. It has four separate sections to take care of—A, B, and C, plus the section to decide what caused the interrupt. That section saves the registers or—to say it another way—"preserves the context of the program to which it must return." Then it scans the peripherals to see what caused the interrupt. Since we have decided that C is more important than B, we should probably test for C first, just in case both interrupts came up at the same time.

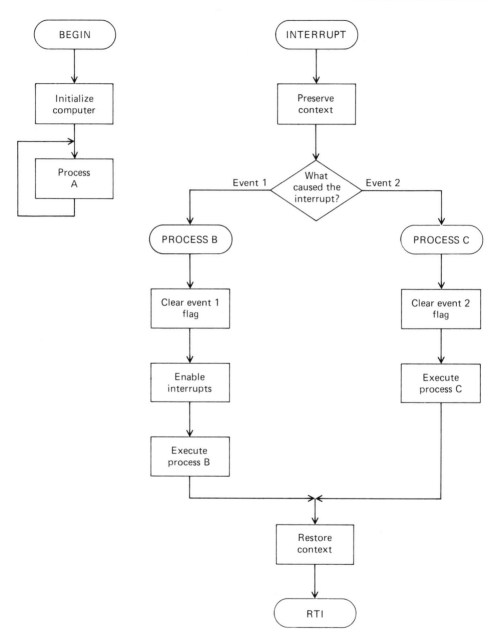

Figures 3.1 *A nested interrupt.*

Process C is just like the interrupt-handling routines we have seen earlier. It carries out its task, restores the context (reloads the registers), and executes an RTI to return to the interrupted program. Process B is slightly different in that we want C to be able to interrupt B, so the first thing B does is turn on the interrupt system (clear the I-bit). Process B then does its work, restores context, and executes an RTI. The initialization routine preceding process A has to take care setting up the I/O ports, the stack, and the I-bit.

We said above that the hardware will save the program counter (and the processor status word) on the stack. We chose to save the A and X registers in main memory at locations named SAVEA and SAVEX. That was a reasonable enough decision at the time, but if we do that now, we are going to get in trouble. Consider. When process A is interrupted by B, it has some numbers in its registers. Call those numbers A_a and X_a. Suppose these are put into SAVEA and SAVEX so that

$$(\text{SAVEA}) = A_a$$
$$(\text{SAVEX}) = X_a$$

Now B in its turn gets interrupted, and at that point B has values A_b and X_b in its registers. If the interrupt routine stores these values in SAVEA and SAVEX, C will be able to return to B with the proper values, but when B tries to return to A, the numbers A_a and X_a have been lost. They were overwritten with A_b and X_b. To avoid this problem, when you have nested interrupts as we have here, you should save the context of the machine on the push-down stack. Code similar to:

PUSHA	Copy contents of Acc *onto* the stack.
PUSHX	Copy contents of X *onto* the stack.

will save the context and

POPX	Copy *out of* stack to X.
POPA	Copy *out of* stack to A.

will restore it. Note that since we pushed X last, that is the first thing we have to pop.

While we are servicing B, the stack will hold:

TOP of stack: X_a
                  A_a
                  PSW_a
                  PC_a

If C interrupts B, we get:

TOP of stack: X_b
                  A_b
                  PSW_b
                  PC_b
                  X_a
                  A_a
                  PSW_a
                  PC_a

stacked up waiting for the restores and returns.

Some machines have many more than two registers, and some machines have a single instruction that will save all the registers on the stack and another single instruction that will restore them. In an 8-bit machine it will take two bytes to hold the PC, and on some machines the PSW is saved before the PC and on others after it. Read your own machine manual to determine what you have.

Exercise 3.1

We are going to simulate a system with two levels of interrupts, using the hardware of Figure 1.14. Let the widget counter invoke process B and the packer's switch invoke process C. In order to determine what the computer is doing, we will let the main routine (process A) generate a tone of approximately 250 cycles per second (hertz). Process B will produce a five-second burst of tone at 300 hertz, and process C will produce a five-second burst of 400 hertz. The exact durations and frequencies are not important as long as they are distinguishable. Representing these three tones as "Hum," "Beep," and "Squeak," we have the following situations:

1. No switch pressed gives a steady "Hummm. . . ."
2. Pressing the widget counter switch alone gives "Hum-m-m Beep Hum-m-m."
3. Pressing the packer's switch alone gives "Hum-m-m Squeak Hum-m-m."
4. Pressing first the widget counter switch and then, while the beep is sounding, pressing the packer's switch gives "Hum-m-m Be-Squeak-ep Hum-m-m."
5. Pressing first the packer's switch and then the widget counter switch should produce "Hum-m-m Squeak Beep Hum-m-m."

Carry out this exercise, and make sure you understand why conditions 4 and 5 give the results they do.

Programming Hints

To generate a tone for five seconds, we need a double loop. Suppose we want to generate 300 Hz. That's 300 vibrations of the speaker cone per second. It goes out 300 times and back in 300 times, causing pressure waves in the air that the ear interprets as sound. To produce this tone, we need to push the speaker cone out, wait 1/600 second, let the speaker cone come back in, wait 1/600 second, and repeat for five seconds. One six-hundredth of a second is approximately 1700 microseconds.

> 250 Hz requires a half period of 2000 microseconds,
> 300 Hz requires a half period of 1700 microseconds, and
> 400 Hz requires a half period of 1250 microseconds.

Let us assume for convenience that a subtract immediately followed by a branch on nonzero accumulator takes up exactly 10 microseconds. Then to generate a 300 Hz tone for five seconds, we need code something like:

SETUP:	LDAIM	1500	Set up the duration counter.
	STA	COUNTER	(Assumes 16-bit machine.)
TONE:	LDAIM	170	
L1:	SUBIM	1	10 microseconds 170 times
	BNA	L1	gives 1700 microseconds.
	LDAIM	1	
	OUTPUT	SPEAKER	Push out speaker cone.
	LDAIM	170	
L2:	SUBIM	1	
	BNA	L2	
	LDAIM	0	
	OUTPUT	SPEAKER	Relax speaker cone.

It will take the computer about 1/300 second to get to here. If we repeat this loop from TONE to this point 1500 times, we will get a duration of five seconds.

	LDA	COUNTER	
	SUBIM	1	Decrement counter.
	STA	COUNTER	
	BNA	TONE	Not done.
	JMP	RESTORE	Yes, we are done.

At restore we will reload the registers and return to the interrupted program. For the sake of simplicity, we have assumed that the number "1500" will fit in the accumulator and a memory cell. If you have an 8-bit machine, you will have to use double-precision arithmetic.

The code for process C is very similar to that for process B. However, we strongly recommend that you do *not* try to conserve typing effort by making B and C use a common subroutine. Wait till you have this running with completely separate code for A, B, and C, and then if you feel you must, go back and rewrite it using subroutines.

Process A is just an endless loop alternately pushing and relaxing the speaker every 2000 microseconds.

MASKING INTERRUPTS

The scheme we have just examined worked because there were only two levels of interrupt: B and C. Suppose now we want to introduce a third level, D, that can interrupt C (and, of course, A and B). We seem to be caught in a dilemma. If C runs with the I-bit set (interrupts inhibited), then D can't interrupt C, but on the other hand, if C runs with the I-bit cleared (interrupts enabled), then B can interrupt C, which is not what we want. To be sure, we could handle this in software by keeping a "level" indicator in memory that kept track of what program was running. Then if B were to interrupt C, we could test in the interrupt identification routine to see if we would allow the new interrupt to take control away from the program presently running. But we would also have to keep track in a word in memory of who had raised interrupts that we have not yet serviced, and we would have to test that word at the conclusion of each interrupt routine. We have to do that, because we must clear the event flag that requests an interrupt. Otherwise, as soon as we clear the I-bit, we will get another interrupt.

While this can be done in software, it is very much simpler if we add the ability to mask interrupts in hardware. Figure 3.2 shows one method of doing this with discrete logic. The two flip-flops are as before, with the first one being used to debounce the switch and the second one to act as the interrupt request flag. But the output of the second flip-flop is ANDed with an additional output bit from the computer called the MASK bit. If the mask bit is one, then the Q_2 output can get through to pull down the IRQ line to 0 and generate an interrupt, but if the mask bit is 0, the event flag (Q_2) is prevented from reaching the IRQ line. It is conventional to provide a mask bit for each possible interrupting event flag and to collect those bits in one or more output registers called the MASK register. The contents of the MASK register(s) become part of the context of the machine and must be saved and restored with the other registers.

Figure 3.3 shows a small mask register with mask bits for event flags B, C, and D. When the main program (A) is running, we will have the pattern 0000 1110 in the mask register. When process B is running, we will have 0000 1100 in the mask register. Process C calls for 0000 1000, and D for all zeros. Thus D can interrupt A, B, or C, C can interrupt A and B, and B can interrupt A. If event flag B gets raised while either C or D is executing, it will not be able to affect the IRQ line, but the flag will still be there sitting at 1. As soon as C or D finishes and tries to go back to process A, the MASK for A will connect the B event flag to the IRQ line and B will get serviced.

We have to be quite careful about the order in which we do things. An interrupt occurs, setting the I-bit to 1 and transferring control to the interrupt identifying routine. First we preserve context. Next we identify which flag caused the interrupt and branch to the proper handler. There we load the mask register with the mask this handler is to run with (we determine who can interrupt this handler).

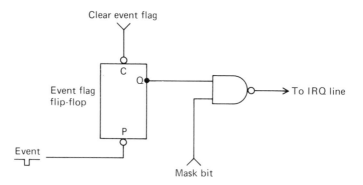

Figure 3.2 *A maskable interrupt. When the mask bit is 0, the event flag cannot pull down the IRQ line.*

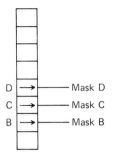

Figure 3.3 *An output port used as a mask register.*

After we load the mask register, we clear the I-bit so that more important processes can interrupt this one. With a mask register such as we have here, one may reorder the priorities of the processes merely by changing the masks that are used.

Exercise 3.2

Connect four push buttons to your computer, as outlined in Figure 3.4. Call these buttons A, B, C, and D. Write a program that will generate a 250-Hz tone for the main program (M) and 300, 400, 500, and 600 Hz, respectively, for processes A, B, C, and D. You will need 9 bits of I/O to make this work: one bit for the speaker, one each for clear A, clear B, clear C, and clear D, plus one each for Mask A, B, C, and D. Experiment with various combinations of buttons to see what sound pat¬ terns you get. Remember that in order for an interrupt to occur the event flag must be set, the mask bit must be 1, and the I-bit must be 0.

HIERARCHICAL INTERRUPTS

One can add a priority encoder to one's external hardware, which will take care of many of the difficulties involved in programming nested interrupts, but in so do-ing, one gives up the flexibility to change priorities by software and must resort to using a soldering iron. The scheme we are about to describe is already wired into a PDP-11 but not into any micro we are aware of.

Figure 3.5 shows an outline of the circuit required. The priority encoder has eight input lines (usually active low) and three output lines. The number that ap-pears on these output lines corresponds to highest numbered input line currently active. Thus, if lines 3 and 6 are active (at 0 volts), the output lines will contain the pattern 110. On some encoders these lines are also active low, so the pattern would be inverted (001). In that case you can insert inverters between these output lines and the comparator. The comparator compares its two input numbers (A and B) and has three output lines (A > B, and A = B, and A < B), which in turn are active high for some chips and active low on others. An active-high A > B line can be con-sidered an active-low B $\geq$ A. We need to develop a line that will pull IRQ to 0 when

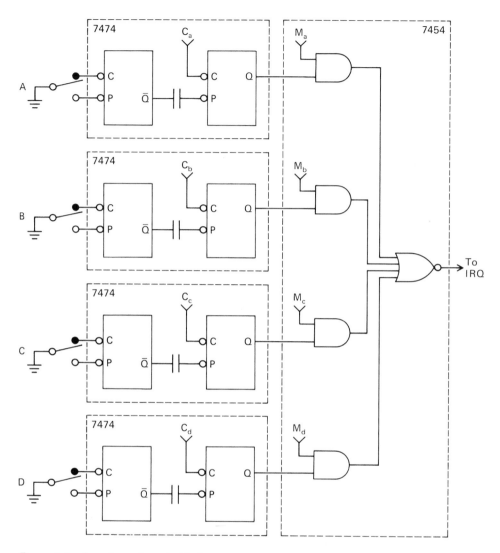

Figure 3.4 *A system of maskable interrupts.*

B is greater than or equal to A. In Figure 3.5, we assume this line is directly available, and its active-low status is indicated by the circle at the output of the comparator.

Now the CPU can set a level at which it wishes to be interrupted in the output register LEVEL, and only when the priority of the event equals or exceeds that level will an interrupt be accepted. A value of 0 in LEVEL will cause the system to respond to any switch, whereas a value of 6 in LEVEL will inhibit switches 0–5 and respond only to switches 6 and 7.

In order to aid the computer in determining which switch caused the interrupt, we bring the output of the priority encoder over to a three-bit input port called

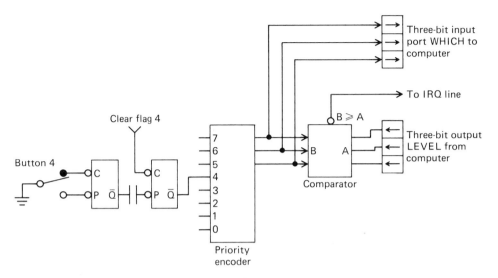

Figure 3.5 *Outline of a priority-encoding scheme.*

WHICH. The interrupt-identifying routine can read this number in and branch on its value to the appropriate handling routine.

A standard way to operate with this hardware might be to save the current value in LEVEL as part of the context, then take the number in WHICH, add one to it, and put it in as a new value in LEVEL. Then turn off the I-bit so that other interrupts of a higher level will be enabled.

VECTORED INTERRUPTS

In most microcomputer systems the NMI, IRQ, and Reset interrupts each send the CPU off to a different location to get the address of the interrupt-handling routine. We talked about the vector address of the IRQ interrupt in Chapter 1. In the system we designed in the last section we do tell the computer who caused the interrupt so that it doesn't have to scan all the control registers looking for a one. But it's up to the software to get to the appropriate handling routine.

It is possible to do better than this if the proper hardware is available. What we want to do is to have a special instruction that will cause the interrupting device to present the CPU with a vector address. Stored at that vector address will be the address of the interrupt-handling routine. For example, when button 1 is asked for its vector, or "trap," address, it responds with "1234." In cells 1234 and 1235 the CPU can find an address of the routine for processing the interrupt caused by button 1.

Suppose the input register from the interrupt hardware is in location F001. Instead of entering the number of the interrupting button into this register, we connect the wires "two to the left" (see Figure 3.6) to give the effect of having "four times the button number" in the register. We arrange that byte F000 contains a byte that decodes as a "jump to page zero" instruction. Now when we want to get to the proper interrupt-handling routine, we jump to location F000. At that location the CPU will find a "jump to page zero, line 4N." Cleverly we have stored in advance a set of jump instructions in cells 0, 4, 8, C, 10, etc. In cells 0, 1, and 2 we have a jump to the handler of interrupt 0. In cells 4, 5, 6 we have a jump to the handler of interrupt 1 (see Figure 3.7).

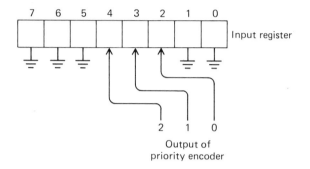

Figure 3.6 *Multiply by 4 the easy way.*

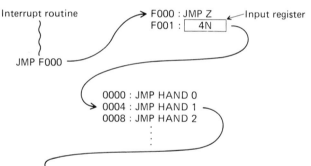

Figure 3.7 *The chain of jumps to get to the proper interrupt handler.*

4 Matching Up Speeds

As soon as a system contains more than one "active" device, it is necessary to synchronize these devices with each other. An active device is one, such as a CPU or a printer or a tape reader, that runs at its own speed and occasionally requires attention or service or interaction with another device. Let us first investigate the classic producer-consumer synchronization problem and then look at how to keep a typewriter and a CPU working together.

SEMAPHORES

Figure 4.1 shows a picture of a producer, a buffer, and a consumer together with two stoplights or semaphores. The semaphore on the left tells the producer whether or not there is room in the buffer to hold another item. As long as there is room in the buffer, the producer will make items and place them in the buffer. When the buffer gets full, the producer will shut down until there is more room. The right-hand semaphore tells the consumer whether or not there are any items in the buffer for it to consume. If there are items, the consumer will consume them. When the buffer becomes empty, the consumer must idle until the producer makes more items.

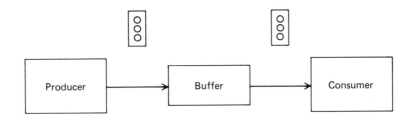

Figure 4.1 *A producer and a consumer.*

The buffer itself has three states: full, partly full, and empty. The producer's stoplight indicates only "full" or "not full" and the consumer's only "empty" or "not empty." In principle this is all there is to the problem, but in practice there are some details that have to be taken care of properly if the system is to operate safely. The major detail involves keeping track of the state of the buffer. Suppose for a moment that the producer and consumer are running on separate CPUs. Let there be a counter that contains the count of the number of items in the buffer that is accessible to both CPUs. The producer compares the count with the size of the buffer, and if COUNT is less than SIZE, it goes ahead and makes another item. It puts this item in the buffer and then adds one to COUNT. The consumer compares COUNT with 0 and, if the number of items is greater than 0, takes an item and subtracts one from COUNT. The problem arises if both producer and consumer try to reference the cell called COUNT at the same time. Suppose both look at COUNT and find it equal to 17. The producer adds one to this number, getting 18, while the consumer subtracts one, getting 16. Now there is a race to see who puts his or her number back first. The first number put into COUNT is immediately overwritten by the second number, and we end up with either 16 or 18 as the value of COUNT. But both of these are wrong. Since we have added one item and subtracted one item, we should end up with the same value, namely, 17.

The way this problem is usually resolved in practice is to invent two "indivisible" instructions called INC and DEC, for "increment by one" and "decrement by one." When executing either of these instructions, the CPU grabs hold of the memory containing COUNT, fetches the value stored there, modifies it, and replaces the new value—all without releasing the memory or permitting interrupts to take place. The reason we want to finish the instruction before releasing memory is so that no other CPU can get to the cell and read out the value stored there until we have replaced the old value with the updated one. Once one CPU starts to change the value stored in COUNT, it must be permitted to finish before any other CPU can reference the cell COUNT. The reason for prohibiting interrupts is that an interrupt routine can behave just like a second CPU. Imagine that the producer is running as an interrupt routine and the consumer as a main routine. If the consumer uses:

```
LDA      COUNT
SUBIM    1
STA      COUNT
```

to record its consuming of an item, it is inevitable that sooner or later the producer will interrupt after the LDA or after the SUBIM. Although the value in the accumulator will be properly preserved over the interrupt, if the interrupting routine changes the number stored in COUNT, that change will get lost when the consumer routine resumes. The DEC instruction's being noninterruptable avoids this problem.

Another way to avoid the problem would be to turn off interrupts while modifying sensitive variables. That will solve the problem for a single CPU with interrupts, but it will not help a multiple CPU at all.

Exercise 4.1

To simulate a producer and consumer, we are going to let the programmer serve as a producer generating inputs to the computer and the computer serve as the consumer.

Use the physical setup of Figure 1.14 under the following interpretation. The producer sees two buttons labeled A and B and a light. Whenever the light is on, there is room in a buffer to accept another button push (either A or B). When the buffer gets full, the light goes out and button pushes are ignored. The consumer, when it senses a nonempty buffer, examines the entry in the buffer. If a push of button A is recorded in the buffer, the consumer generates a five-second tone of 300 Hz. If a push of button B is recorded, the consumer generates a five-second tone of 400 Hz. When the consumer finishes outputting a tone, it removes that entry from the buffer. Let the buffer have room for five entries.

Programming Hints

The first thing we need is what is called a "circular buffer." Let the buffer run from cell BEGIN to cell END inclusive, and let there be two pointers called PUTIN and TAKEOUT. The producer uses PUTIN as a pointer to the slot in the buffer where it should store the next item it generates. It stores a new item in the slot pointed at by PUTIN and then adds one to the pointer in PUTIN. If the new value in PUTIN is greater than END (you are pointing past the end of the buffer), then the address of BEGIN is placed in PUTIN (the pointer is reset to the beginning of the buffer). The same circular addressing scheme is used for TAKEOUT. TAKEOUT will point to the next cell to be read by the consumer (see Figure 4.2).

When TAKEOUT catches up with PUTIN, the buffer is empty. When PUTIN catches up with TAKEOUT, the buffer is full. The least complicated way to control the operations of the producer and the consumer is to use an additional variable called COUNT. We will make the producer be interrupt-driven by interrupts generated by pushes of buttons 1 and 2. The consumer will constitute the main program.

When a button is pushed, the producer examines COUNT. If COUNT equals 5, indicating that the buffer is full, the producer turns off the light (it may already be off), clears the interrupt—thus discarding it—and returns to the main program.

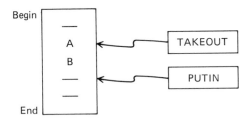

Figure 4.2 *A circular buffer containing entries "A" and "B."*

If COUNT is less than 5, the producer stores the entry (1 or 2) in the cell pointed at by PUTIN, increments PUTIN with wrap-around, and increments COUNT by one. Then it clears the interrupt and returns.

The consumer sits in a tight loop, watching the value in COUNT. As long as that value is 0, the consumer continues to loop. When the value in COUNT is not 0, the consumer reads out an item from the cell pointed at by TAKEOUT. Next, it increments TAKEOUT with wrap-around, decrements COUNT by 1, and turns on the light, indicating to the programmer that the buffer is not full. After completing these operations, the consumer goes off to generate the appropriate tone for five seconds, after which it comes back to check COUNT again. If you have two or more timers connected to your computer, it might be instructive to use them to generate the tone and to control its duration. If these timers generate interrupts at the end of each time period, you will have a respectably complicated interrupt system to deal with and some decisions to make about whether you should run interrupts with the I-bit set or cleared. Since all four handling routines (the two buttons and the two timers) are quite short, it is possible and probably preferable to leave the I-bit set while servicing an interrupt, but it would be good experience to do it the other way.

HANDSHAKING

The peripheral interface adapters (PIAs) of Chapter 2 have been designed to facilitate the interfacing of peripheral devices with a CPU. In this section we are going to examine how a CPU, a PIA, and a typewriter might be connected together.

In the previous section we looked at how semaphores worked. If the buffer size is reduced to exactly one, things become somewhat simpler. First of all, there is no need for the pointers PUTIN and TAKEOUT, since the address of the single cell of the buffer can be referenced directly. Second, the variable COUNT reduces to a logical variable with only two states—0 = empty and 1 = full, with consequently simplified testing. Such logical variables are often called "flags," and we will use them to synchronize the CPU and the typewriter.

A typewriter usually consists of two independent devices: a printing mechanism and a keyboard. When this is so, the typewriter is said to be operating in "full duplex" mode. A key stroke on the keyboard goes into the computer and then, via software intervention, back out to the printer in order to record the key stroke as a character on paper. If the CPU were turned off, the typewriter would not work at all in this mode.

KEYBOARD

We will consider a keyboard connected to the A side of a 6520 PIA. We will take this in stages getting more complicated as we go. First, we will assume that the keyboard is of the "encoded" type with 8-bit parallel output plus a line that goes to logical 1 whenever any key is depressed (see Figure 4.3). This "some key" line is connected to I_{1A}, and control register bits $C_1 C_0$ are set to 11 so that when the some-key line goes to 1, bit C_7 is set and LIRQA (and hence IRQ) gets pulled to 0. Since

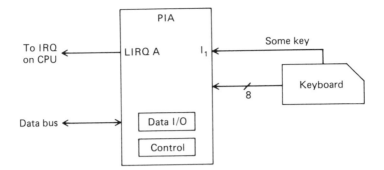

Figure 4.3 *A typewriter keyboard connected directly to a PIA.*

the striking of keys is not under computer control, we do not connect anything to I_{2A}. When a key is struck, the ASCII representation of that key is placed in the I/O register, C_7 is set, and an interrupt is generated. The CPU scans its peripherals to determine what caused the interrupt. It finds C_7 set, indicating that it was this peripheral, so it reads the I/O register to get the character. Reading the I/O register automatically clears C_7 and allows LIRQA and hence IRQ to return to 1.

Now consider the case in which the typewriter keyboard is a bit serial device. Assume it sends one start bit (logical 0) eight information bits and a single stop bit (logical 1). In Figure 4.4 we insert a UART between the keyboard and the computer. One of the standard methods of connection is called a "20-milliamp loop." When no information is being transmitted, a steady 20ma current flows along the line returning through ground. This is shown as a twisted pair of wires. The first thing the keyboard sends out is a "start pulse," which is represented by an absence of current. This is followed by eight equal-time intervals during which there is or is not current flowing. The 256 possible patterns of eight yes or no current intervals encode the characters of the keyboard, each key producing a different pattern. Finally, the keyboard sends a "stop pulse," which is represented by the presence of current. Some older keyboards send two stop pulses. Together these 10 or 11 pulses represent a character.

The UART detects the absence of current, representing the start pulse. It clears its first receiver buffer, RB, and starts its interior clock to tell it when to sample the input line so that it can capture the eight approaching information pulses. When the last information pulse is captured, the UART copies the pattern from RB to RA and pulls down the IRQ line.

In Figure 4.5 we show an unencoded keyboard. Assume that there are 64 keys on the keyboard. These are arranged as eight rows of 8. At the intersections of rows and columns there are 64 switches, which connect a row with a column when that key is pressed. Each row has a 10,000-ohm (10K) resistor connecting it to plus 5 volts so that when no key is pressed, the input port ROW sees all 1's. (These resistors are not strictly necessary if TTL input ports are used, because they tend to "drift" to plus 5 if no input is supplied, but without them there may be a problem of noise, giving false signals.)

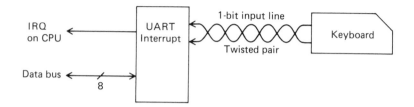

Figure 4.4 *A bit serial typewriter connected through a UART.*

The output port is left containing all 0's, and when any key is depressed, its row is connected to a 0, and both that bit of ROW and the input to the NAND circuit ("Not AND" has an output of 1 if any of its inputs are 0) are pulled to 0. The output of the NAND is connected to I_{1A} of the PIA. The A control register bits 1 and 0 ($C_{1A} C_{0A}$) contain the pattern 11 so that when the output of the NAND goes to 1, C_{7A} is set and the LIRQA line is pulled to 0. If LIRQA is connected to the IRQ line of the CPU, an interrupt will be generated.

The CPU can tell it was a keyboard interrupt from the fact that C_{7A} is at 1, but now it must scan the eight columns to find out which key was depressed. It does this by putting the patterns

$$
\begin{array}{cc}
0111 & 1111 \\
1011 & 1111 \\
1101 & 1111 \\
1110 & 1111 \\
1111 & 0111 \\
1111 & 1011 \\
1111 & 1101 \\
1111 & 1110 \\
\end{array}
$$

into the register COLUMN, one after another, and seeing which pattern causes the input port ROW to have a 0 in it. Then, from a knowledge of which column caused a 0 and which row the 0 was in, it can identify the key that was pressed. The combination of row and column number can be used directly as a key identifier, or that combination can be used as an index into a table to retrieve the ASCII representation of the key.

The PIA is used to provide two registers and also to uncouple the NAND output from direct contact with the IRQ line. The user may hold a key down for some time, and we don't want to keep on being interrupted by the same key stroke. We could uncouple the NAND, as we did the push buttons of earlier chapters, but we would then need another output bit to clear the interrupt (remember the PIA clears C_{7A} whenever we read ROW), and we would still need two 8-bit I/O ports (8 out for COLUMN and 8 in for ROW).

We can reduce the number of I/O bits required if we employ multiplexers and demultiplexers, as shown in Figure 4.6. A multiplexer (MUX) has eight input lines,

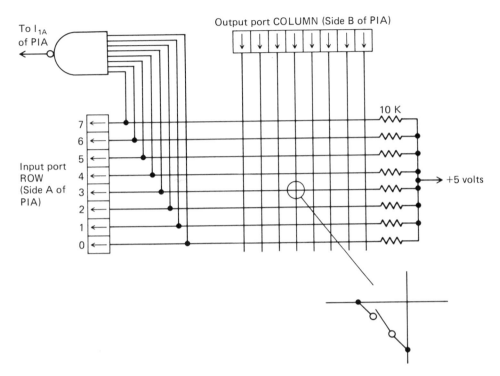

Figure 4.5 *An unencoded 64-key keyboard. A key is connected at each intersection.*

one output line, and three selector lines. Depending on the pattern on the selector lines, one of the input lines is connected to the output line. Such a chip is used to connect the row lines to bit 7 of the I/O port. Bits 6, 5, and 4 control which row is connected to bit 7.

A demultiplexer (DEMUX) performs the inverse function. Under control of the selector lines, one of the outputs is connected to the input line. Depending on which DEMUX you are employing, the other seven output lines are allowed to go to plus 5 volts (usually) or to 0 volts (sometimes).

An interrupt for this scheme could be generated the same way as was done in Figure 4.5, provided the DEMUX you select lets the unconnected output lines go to plus 5 volts. This general scheme has the disadvantage that we must scan both rows and columns in a double loop. It will consequently be quite slow. Furthermore, it is not immediately clear that by the time you buy one I/O port and a MUX and a DEMUX you wouldn't be better off getting a PIA in the first place. We include it for the sake of completeness.

PRINTER

Let us now look briefly at how to connect a typewriter printing mechanism to a computer using a PIA. Figure 4.7 shows this. We use the B side of a 6520 PIA, because that side is designed for output handshaking.

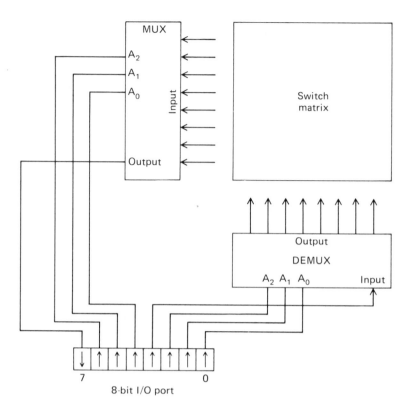

Figure 4.6 *Use of a MUX and a DEMUX to partially encode a keyboard.*

At initialization time we set the direction register for B to be all output, and then we load the pattern

$$\text{value} \quad 1 \; 0 \; 1 \; 1 \; 0 \; 1$$
$$\text{bits} \quad \; 5 \; 4 \; 3 \; 2 \; 1 \; 0$$

into control register B. The 101 in C_{5B}–C_{3B} causes I_{2B} to generate a brief pulse whenever the I/O port B register is written into by the CPU. This pulse is fed to the printer to begin printing the character it sees on the eight information lines from I/O port B.

When the printer finishes, it pulls the busy line to 0. Because $C_1 \, C_0$ contain 01 when BUSY goes to 0, LIRQB is pulled to 0 and the CPU is interrupted. The CPU gets another character and stores it in I/O port B, which starts the whole process off again.

We chose to use the B side of the PIA so that we could automatically pulse I_{2B} when we loaded the I/O port without having to program it. Writing in the I/O register also clears C_{7B} and releases LIRQB, clearing the interrupt. Now perhaps we can begin to see why the PIA was designed the way it was to simplify just this sort of operation.

MULTIPLEXER — DEMULTIPLEXER

Again there are many multiplexers and demultiplexers available in the 74XX series and in other series as well. We will present only two here, both 8-way devices.

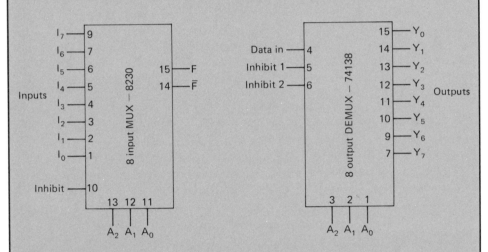

The 8230 multiplexer connects one of the eight input lines I_0–I_7 to the output line F. Which input is selected is determined by the address lines A_2–A_0. When the inhibit line is high, the output F is high, regardless of the state of the selected input line. $\overline{F}$ is the complement of F.

The 74138 demultiplexer connects the "data in" line to one of the output lines selected by A_2–A_0. When either inhibit line is 1, all outputs are high. When both inhibit lines are low, the unselected outputs are high, and the selected output line follows the "data in" line.

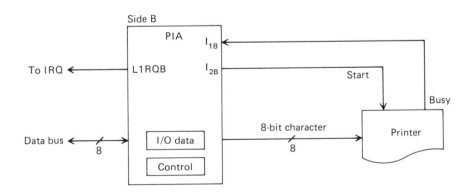

Figure 4.7 *Connection of a printer to a computer via a PIA.*

THE IEEE-488 BUS

Another example of handshaking for the transfer of data occurs on the IEEE-488 bus. This 488 bus is an official standard for communication of information. It is implemented on the PET 2001 from Commodore and will probably appear on other microcomputer systems in the future.

The standard describes a common interface for control devices and for sources and sinks of information. At any one time there is exactly one controller on the bus. This controller selects "talkers" (sources) and "listeners" (sinks), and then it allows the talker to communicate with the listeners. There may be only one talker active at a time, but there may be several listeners. The slowest active listener controls the rate of transfer.

Information is transmitted one 8-bit byte at a time. The physical bus consists of 16 signal lines divided into three sets of lines called "data," "manager," and "transfer." All these lines are active low (true when 0). There are eight data lines named DIO 1 through DIO 8 (data input output 1–8) with DIO 8 being the most significant bit. There are five manager lines that are involved with management of the bus and with the transfer of control. These are:

EOI — End of information, may be set low by the talker during the transfer of the last byte of information.

IFC — Interface clear causes all devices to assume inactive status (cease being talkers and listeners).

SRC — Service request, an interruptlike line asserted by devices other than the controller.

REN — Remote enable, held at ground if the CPU is to be the only controller.

ATN — Attention.

The ATN line is used to distinguish messages to devices from data. Messages to devices include peripheral addresses and control information. When ATN is true (low), information on the data lines is a message—perhaps to assume talker status or rewind a tape. When ATN is false (high), the data lines are used to transmit data.

Any communication between the CPU and a peripheral device begins with an attention sequence that activates the device and prepares it for the transfer. This is equivalent to an OPEN FILE command in a higher-level language and indeed is implemented as such in PET BASIC. When the transfer of information is complete, it should be followed by an attention sequence that deactivates the device (closes the file).

The three lines of the transfer group are:

DAV — Data valid—set true (low) by the talker when valid data is present on the data lines.

NRFD — Not ready for data—set true (low) when a listener is not ready to accept data.

NDAC — Not data accepted—set by a listener.

Figure 4.8 shows the use of these lines. As each listener becomes ready to accept data, it releases the NRFD line, which is pulled high by a resistor. When all listeners are ready, no device is holding the NRFD down, so it goes high. Meanwhile, the current talker has put data on the data lines. When the talker senses NRFD high, indicating that all listeners are ready, and after it has put data on the data lines and allowed them to settle, the talker asserts that data is valid and that a transfer should take place by pulling DAV low.

As each listener detects DAV low, it pulls NRFD low to indicate that it is in the process of capturing the data. The fastest listener will be the one to pull NRFD low, and it will stay low until the slowest listener has digested this byte of data and is again ready for data. As each listener absorbs the data, it releases NDAC. When the last listener has accepted the data, NDAC is pulled high by a resistor.

The talker sees NDAC high and sets DAV high, indicating that it is about to change information on the bus. The listeners see DAV go high, so they all pull NDAC low, indicating that "data is not accepted." Now the listeners have absorbed the data, so the bus can be changed, because it is not needed just now for communication, but the listeners may not yet have finished storing the data in their memory—or if one listener is a printer, it may not have finished the print cycle. When each listener in turn becomes ready to accept new data, it releases NRFD. When the last listener is ready, the cycle starts again and a new byte can be transferred.

Many laboratory instruments, voltmeters, electronic thermometers, and recording devices are available built to interface on the 488 bus. As home computers begin to deal with more sophisticated measuring devices, the use of this bus will become more widespread.

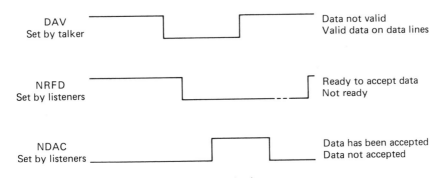

Figure 4.8 *Timing sequence of the three transfer lines.*

5 Echo and Reverberation

Contemporary electric guitarists are interested in ways of modifying the sounds that their instruments produce. They add "fuzz" and "wah" and tremulo and vibrato and reverberation and echo and flangers and phasers and octave doublers and dividers. All of these effects can be generated with a digital computer, and in this chapter and the next we are going to investigate a few of them.

In this chapter we are going to look at how to build a reverberation-echo unit with a microcomputer, but as usual, we first have to learn some other things.

ECHO

To create an echo, one needs to record a sound and play it back a fraction of a second later. If the time of storage is long enough—say, about a second—we usually call it an echo. If the time of storage and delay is shorter, perhaps a twentieth or fortieth of a second, we call it reverberation, after the closely spaced bouncing sounds we hear in a large bare room. If a single pluck of a guitar string goes "PLINK . . . plink," that's a single echo. If it goes "PLINK, PLINk, PLInk, PLink . . . ," that's reverberation.

We are going to measure the input sound wave once every 50 microseconds. We will discuss how to measure it a bit later. If the note being played has a frequency of 1000 Hertz, then we will be able to get 20 samples of the wave form per cycle (per millisecond). Figure 5.1 shows the original sound wave at A, the samples we take at B, and the digitized output we are going to generate at C. The output consists of a series of steplike values. When we take a sample of the original signal, we will output the value we just measured until we have a new value to put out. This leads to the flat tops of the stairs.

We are not going to be able to measure the input with infinite resolution or to generate an arbitrary output with infinite resolution either. Since most microcomputers are byte-oriented machines, we will arrange to store our estimate of the

60

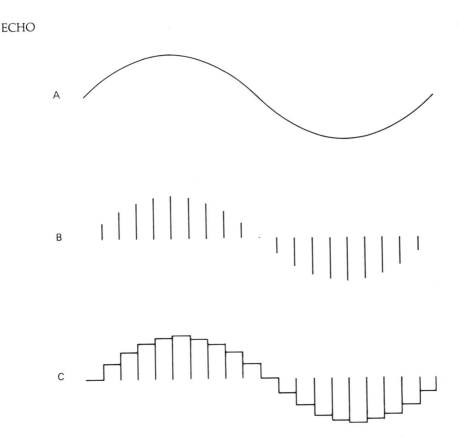

Figure 5.1 *A sine wave at A is sampled 20 times per cycle at B, and it reproduces as a series of steps of constant magnitude at C.*

input in one byte. This means it can take on at most 256 values. These values could be used to represent voltages between zero and 5 volts, with zero being zero and 5 volts being represented by 255 (called unsigned binary), or they could be used to represent excursions either side of zero, say, plus or minus 2.5 volts (called signed binary). In addition to a choice between signed and unsigned binary, we can choose what full-scale value we wish to have. That is whether the bit pattern FF should represent 1 volt or 17.5 volts or, indeed, 110 volts. Suppose for the moment we choose unsigned binary with full scale equal to 10 volts. Now any voltage, V, in the range from 0 to 10 volts will be represented by a binary number N, where

$$N = 255 * \frac{V}{10}.$$

Let $N = 128$. Then V will have been $(128 \times 10)/255 = 5.0196$. The next larger value N can take on is 129, which represents a voltage of $(129 \times 10)/255 = 5.0588$. Thus the mimimum change in the input that will generate a change in the sample is roughly 0.04 volts full scale or one part in 255 (which we might have been able to predict with a little thought). This minimum change is called the "quantization noise" and is present whenever we convert between analog and digital signals.

Measuring a sample to greater resolution requires using more bits to measure the sample. This is often done when fine detail is desired, and 10, 12, 16, or even 18 bits (one part in 262,144) can be achieved.

Suppose we store the samples as we get them in a circular buffer. That's a buffer in which we write information into successive cells until we come to the end of the buffer, and then we start over again at the beginning. (See Exercise 4.1 in Chapter 4.) In mathematical terms we "address the buffer *modulo* its size." Let the buffer have N cells, and let us write into the buffer once every T microseconds. Then the cell we are just about to write into was last written into $T \cdot N$ microseconds ago. So the information stored there is $T \cdot N$ microseconds old. If $T = 50$ and $N = 1000$, then the information is 50,000 microseconds or 1/20 second old. That's comparable to the reverberation time of a room 25 feet on a side. Not exactly the Astrodome but a bit larger than the average closet.

A program for accomplishing the above would not be very complicated; we will show just the mainloop in Figure 5.2.

Beginning at LOOP, we output the old signal at DELAY and then read in a new signal, store it in the buffer, and also output it at PROMPT. An external potentiometer, as shown in Figure 5.3, will be ideal to mix the two signals in any desired proportions.

Let us return to the original problem. We want to generate an effect called reverberation. This is similar to the echoes one might get in a cave where each word or sound is heard many times as it bounces from wall to wall, only gradually dying away to silence. To do this we are going to put a sound into our delay unit. When it comes out the other end (some time later), we will take a large fraction of the sound, mix it with new incoming sounds, and put it back into the delay unit. This way a loud sound will go through the delay unit many times before it finally grows too soft to hear. Figure 5.4 shows the heart of such a program.

```
HOLD:   NOP
        NOP              We come here to waste some time, so two
        NOP              paths are equal.
LOOP:   LDAX   BUFFER    Get the old level.
        OUTPUT DELAY     Output at port "DELAY."
        INPUT  SIGNAL    Get the new input signal.
        STAX   BUFFER    Put it into buffer.
        OUTPUT PROMPT    And output at port "PROMPT."
        INX              Increment the index register.
        TXA              Transfer value in X to accumulator.
        SUBIM  256
        BMA    HOLD      Go to HOLD if X < 256.
        LDXIM  0         Reset index register to zero.
        JMP    LOOP
```

Figure 5.2 *A program to provide a delayed signal at DELAY and an undelayed signal at PROMPT.*

Figure 5.3 *A diagram of the connections required for the program of Figure 5.2. The signals at DELAY and PROMPT are mixed to provide the output desired with little echo (potentiometer near bottom) or strong echo (potentiometer near middle).*

The new signal from GUITAR is put out immediately at the port labeled PROMPT. Then half of the new signal is added to half of what used to be in the Xth slot of the buffer (that's the old signal from one full delay time ago) and placed back in BUFFER(X). Each time we get back to this buffer slot, we will divide the remaining old signal by two. This represents a fairly strongly damped room, one with rugs, drapes, and other such sound-absorbing material in it. Perhaps the guitarist would prefer a more cavelike reverberation. In that case he must keep more of the old signal each time it comes out of the delay unit.

What he must do is take the new input, add it to the old signal in some proportion, and then save the resulting sum in the buffer. For example,

$$B' = aI + bB,$$

where B' is the new buffer signal, B is the old, I is the input, and a and b are multipliers. If b is much larger than a, there will be lots of reverberation, because we are keeping most of the old signal and relatively little of the new. Assuming that the largest possible value for the input I will fit in one byte ($-128 \leqslant I \leqslant 127$), we seek first a constraint on a and b such that the signal to be stored in the buffer never overflows. That constraint is easily satisfied if

$$a + b \leqslant 1,$$

```
LOOP:   LDAX     BUFFER       Divide the number in
        ASR                   BUFFER (X) by two.
        STA      TEMP
        INPUT    GUITAR       Get new signal.
        OUTPUT   PROMPT
        ASR                   Divide it by two.
        ADD      TEMP         Add in delayed signal.
        STAX     BUFFER       Put it back in BUFFER(X).
        OUTPUT   DELAY        Output it at port DELAY.
```

Figure 5.4 *A loop that will give a reverberation effect. We assume that index register X is pointing to the oldest slot in the buffer.*

and we will select the equality for our design. Note that in Figure 5.4 by a strange coincidence we had $a = b = 1/2$. Should you fail to believe in that constraint, relax it and assume $a = b = 3/4$ and that you have a constant input of $I = 1$. What happens to B?

If your computer has a hardware multiply instruction, you may choose a and b to be any convenient values and proceed without further problems. But suppose your machine does not have a multiply instruction. Are you completely out of luck?

LIMITED BUT QUICK MULTIPLICATIONS

A general multiplication subroutine that will perform multiplication of any two 8-bit bytes will run much too slowly for our purposes. We have already seen in Figure 5.4 that multiplication by a half is quite fast. So, too, is multiplication by a quarter or an eighth or a sixteenth. Given this, we can rapidly form products that are representable by:

$$V \cdot \left(1 - \frac{1}{2^m}\right).$$

For example, $3/4$ of the variable V can be found quickly and neatly by:

```
LDA    V              Get V.
ASR
ASR                   Find V/4.
STA    TEMP
LDA    V              V
SUB    TEMP           -1/4V = 3/4V.
```

and Figure 5.5 shows a reverberation program in which $a = 1/16$, $b = 15/16$.

OUTPUT—DIGITAL TO ANALOG CONVERSION

To generate sound for our guitarist to listen to, we need to convert our digital numbers into voltages that will drive his amplifiers. Suppose we have a signal of some sort and we wish to put it out from the computer in a continuous as opposed to a discrete form. That is, we don't just want a light to be on or off (digital output); we want to be able to vary the intensity of the light in a more or less continuous fashion from *off* through *dim* to *bright*.

The first and least expensive way of generating an analog output is via a scheme that has been named the variable duty-cycle DAC (digital to analog converter). Suppose the number stored in the variable VALUE has a range from zero to 255. We are going to set up a loop that will count down on a variable called TEMP from 255 to zero and then do it all over again. While the count in TEMP is greater than VALUE, we will output a zero. If the count is less than VALUE, we will output a logical one. The nearer VALUE is to zero, the smaller a percentage of

```
LOOP:    INPUT     INPORT
         OUTPUT    PROMPT  ⎫
         ARS               ⎪
         ARS               ⎪
         ARS               ⎬   TAKE 1/16 of I.
         ARS               ⎪
         STA       TEMP1   ⎭
         LDAX      BUFFER  ⎫
         ARS               ⎪
         ARS               ⎪
         ARS               ⎬   Take 1/16 of BUFFER.
         ARS               ⎪
         STA       TEMP2   ⎭
         LDAX      BUFFER  ⎫   Get 15/16 of BUFFER.
         SUB       TEMP2   ⎭
         ADD       TEMP1
         STAX      BUFFER
         OUTPUT    DELAY
         INX                   Increment X.
         JMP       LOOP
```

Figure 5.5 *Reverberation. Form the value $(\frac{1}{16} * I + \frac{5}{16} * BUFFER)$. We assume that X is an 8-bit register and that the buffer is 256 cells long.*

the time will we put out a one. In fact, the percentage of ones we put out will be exactly proportional to the number in VALUE divided by 255 (see Figure 5.6). Figure 5.7 shows the wave form generated by the algorithm of Figure 5.6, and Figure 5.8 shows a smoothing circuit for that wave form. This smoothing circuit is present to eliminate spurious high frequencies from the output signal. We will discuss such circuits more fully in Chapter 7.

The RC time constant (the product of the size of the resistor in ohms and the size of the capacitor in farads) should be long compared with the period of the wave form. Since the minimum time around the loop will be of the order of 20 microseconds, we have a minimum period of around 5 milliseconds.

This is very much too slow to be of use in generating tones in the audible range. We need something like 200 times this speed to handle sounds up to 20,000 Hertz (the limit of hearing). To get the time of conversion (from digital to analog form) down to a few microseconds, we need to go to a "ladder DAC." Here, instead of averaging across time as we did with the variable duty cycle DAC, we will average many separate signals. Imagine for a moment 255 resistors, each of exactly 100,000 ohms, connected to 255 output bits from the computer with their other ends all tied together to a common point. Now if N of these output bits are one and the remaining $255 - N$ are zero, the common point to which all these resistors are

AN INEXPENSIVE VOLTMETER

If you are going to be doing any amount of circuit construction at all, it is well worthwhile to invest in an inexpensive voltmeter. You do not need a meter of high accuracy, and you certainly don't need to go to the expense of a digital meter. Nor do you need a lot of scales. Most of the time you are going to be measuring DC voltages between 0 and 5 volts, so a meter with a full-scale reading of 6 or 10 volts would be ideal. If you want to use it around the house for general electrical work, then an AC scale capable of accommodating 120 V would be very useful.

You don't need high-frequency response on the AC measurements. Most inexpensive meters work admirably for frequencies below 10,000 Hz, and that is more than enough.

Many meters are rated at a sensitivity of "20,000 ohms per volt" somewhere on the face of the meter. This means that for 10 volts full scale the meter has a resistance of 200,000 ohms, which really means that the meter will draw 50 microamps when the needle is deflected to a full-scale reading. Other meters are rated at 10,000 ohms per volt, at 5000, and some at 1000 ohms per volt. If you have a choice, get the highest ohms per volt that you can afford. The less current the meter draws (the higher its rating), the less it will act as a load on the thing it is trying to measure. Probably 5000 ohms per volt is as low as you should go.

Most voltmeters include some current measuring scales. In general, the more of those the better, but don't sacrifice sensitivity to get current scales. They are not that useful.

```
BEGIN:      LDAIM     255          Begin with TEMP = 255.
            STA       TEMP
LOOP:       LDA       TEMP
            SUBIM     1            Subtract 1 from TEMP.
            STA       TEMP
            SUBIM     VALUE        Compare TEMP with VALUE.
            BMA       LESS
GREATER:    LDAIM     0            TEMP ≥ VALUE.
            OUTPUT    OUTPORT      OUTPUT 0.
            JMP       LOOP
LESS:       LDAIM     1            TEMP < VALUE.
            OUTPUT    OUTPORT      OUTPUT 1.
            JMP       LOOP
```

Figure 5.6 *A variable duty cycle DAC. Assumes BMA takes a constant time, whether or not it executes the jump.*

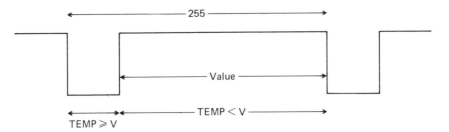

Figure 5.7 *The wave form generated by the algorithm of Figure 5.6.*

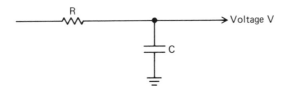

Figure 5.8 *A smoothing circuit for the algorithm of Figure 5.6.*

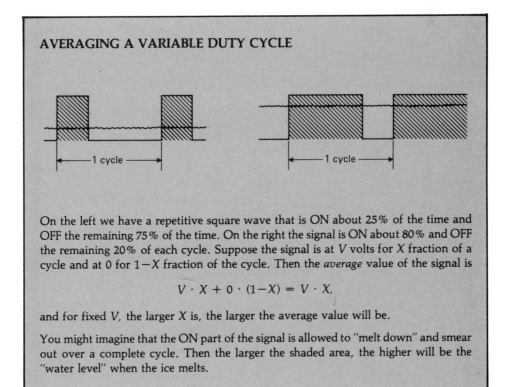

AVERAGING A VARIABLE DUTY CYCLE

On the left we have a repetitive square wave that is ON about 25% of the time and OFF the remaining 75% of the time. On the right the signal is ON about 80% and OFF the remaining 20% of each cycle. Suppose the signal is at V volts for X fraction of a cycle and at 0 for $1-X$ fraction of the cycle. Then the *average* value of the signal is

$$V \cdot X + 0 \cdot (1-X) = V \cdot X,$$

and for fixed V, the larger X is, the larger the average value will be.

You might imagine that the ON part of the signal is allowed to "melt down" and smear out over a complete cycle. Then the larger the shaded area, the higher will be the "water level" when the ice melts.

connected will assume a voltage that is $N/255$ times the value of a logical one. To prove that the voltage at the junction of the resistors is what we desire, we proceed as follows.

The amount of current that will flow through a resistor is proportional to the voltage across it. The potential the common point assumes, V, will be such that there is as much current flowing in as flowing out. That is, we don't get any buildup in the number of electrons at that point. Suppose there are X resistors connected to plus 5 volts and $255-X$ connected to zero volts. Balancing currents in and out, we have

$$(5-V)X = V(255-X)$$

or

$$V = 5 \cdot \frac{X}{255} \cdot$$

VOLTS, OHMS, AND AMPERES

To program a computer you don't need to know a thing about electricity, but to deal with I/O in any detail you must know at least some fundamentals.

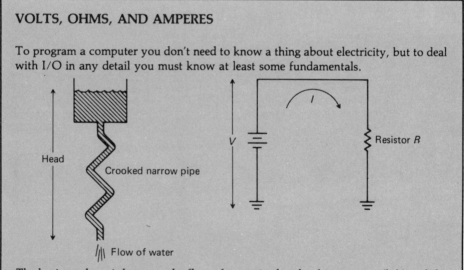

The basic analogy is between the flow of water in the plumbing system (left) and the flow of current in the electrical circuit (right). The greater the head of water (the higher the water level is above the exit point), the faster the water will flow out of the tank. The narrower and more crooked the pipe is, the slower the water will go out. The head of water (the water pressure) corresponds to the voltage, V. The flow of water corresponds to the flow of current, I, and the narrow crooked pipe to the resistor, R. The higher the voltage applied, the higher the current. The larger the resistance, R, the smaller the current. These three quantities are related by the equation known as Ohm's law:

$$V = I \cdot R,$$

where V is measured in volts, I in amperes, and R in ohms. One volt will cause one ampere to flow through a resistance of one ohm.

PARALLEL AND SERIES

If we have two resistors, R_1 and R_2, we can connect them together in parallel

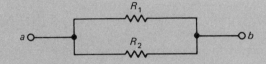

or in series

Let there be a voltage, V, established between points a and b. Each resistor will pass a certain amount of current, as determined by Ohm's law:

$$I_1 = \frac{V}{R_1} \qquad I_2 = \frac{V}{R_2}.$$

Then the total current flowing between a and b will be $I_1 + I_2$, or

$$\frac{V}{R_1} + \frac{V}{R_2} = V\left(\frac{1}{R_1} + \frac{1}{R_2}\right),$$

but this is the same current that would flow if we replaced the two parallel resistors by a single resistor, R_p, whose size is given by:

$$R_p = \frac{1}{1/R_1 + 1/R_2} = \frac{R_1 \cdot R_2}{R_1 + R_2}.$$

When resistors are placed in series, their resistances will add to each other. So if R_1 and R_2 are put in series, they could be replaced by a single resistor, R_s, of magnitude

$$R_s = R_1 + R_2.$$

If $R_1 = R_2$, these equations simplify to

$$R_p = 1/2\, R_1 \qquad R_s = 2\, R_1.$$

But this arrangement of identical resistors gives us freedoms we don't want *or* need. For example, if $N = 128$, we could set the first 128 bits to one or the last 128 or the even-numbered bits or any other pattern we choose, just so the total comes out to 128.

Let us remove that freedom by connecting our 255 resistors in eight batches, as shown in Figure 5.9. To get exactly N resistors connected to logical one, there is only one pattern of bits 0–7 that will suffice, namely, the pattern that is the binary

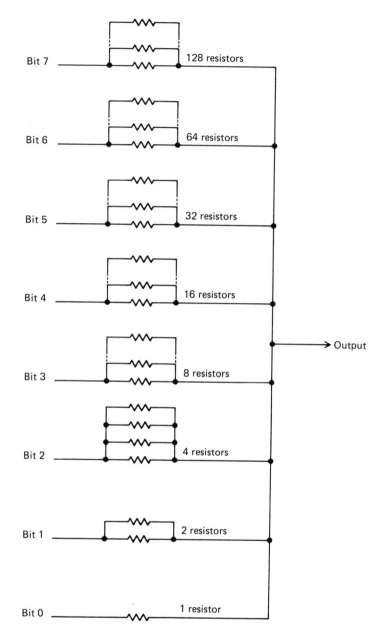

Figure 5.9 *The set of 255 resistors connected in batches.*

representation of the number N. We can simplify the circuit of Figure 5.8 considerably by noting that N identical resistors tied in parallel have a net resistance to the flow of current that is $1/N$ times as large as one of the resistors alone. So we can replace the 128 resistors of 100,000 ohms each by one resistor of 781¼ ohms.

The 64 resistors in parallel connected to bit 6 become 1562½ ohms, etc. Since these odd values might be a bit hard to find, let us scale everything up so that the resistor connected to bit 7 is exactly 1000 ohms, and the others are, in order, 2K, 4K, 8K, 16K, 32K, 64K, and 128K.

There are several other kinds of high-speed digital to analog converters. Next most popular after the ladder type is one called an "R–2R network" (see Figure 5.10). At (a) we show two resistors in parallel. Since they are equal, any current coming into point A will divide equally between the two paths. Further, since both resistors have a value of 2R, they may be replaced (conceptually) by a single resistor of value R. Now look at Figure 5.10(b). The two 2R resistors on the right have a resistance of R. That resistance is in series with another resistor of size R, so paths 2 and 3 combined present a resistance of $R+R = 2R$ from point B to ground. But now point B sees the same situation as point A of Figure 5.10(a), namely, two paths to ground (path 1 and path 23 combined), each of value 2R. So any current coming into B from the left divides in half here, and further, point B presents a resistance of R to ground.

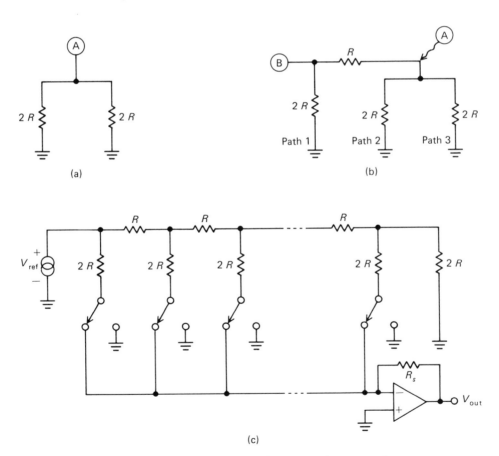

Figure 5.10 *An R–2R network and a DAC built using such a network.*

Now look at Figure 5.10(c). On the left is a reference voltage, V_{ref}. It sees a resistance to ground of R and consequently delivers a current of

$$I_{in} = \frac{V_{ref}}{R}.$$

I_{in} splits, one half going down the first $2R$ resistor and the other half going to the right. At the next junction the same thing happens, half of the half of I_{in} going down the $2R$ resistor and the other half of the half going right. So the set of $2R$ resistors have currents flowing through them of size $1/2\ I_{in}$, $1/4\ I_{in}$, $1/8\ I_{in}$, ...

At the bottom end of the $2R$ resistors we show switches. It is to be understood that these are high-speed electronic switches, not mechanical ones. Each switch is controlled by one bit of the digital output signal and switches the current coming down the $2R$ resistor either to ground (when the bit is 0) or to the summing input of the amplifier (the triangle) when the bit is 1.

The summing amplifier has a high gain and, connected as shown in Figure 5.9(c), will do its best to keep its input terminal at ground potential. To do this it increases its output voltage until the current flowing through R_s is just equal and opposite to the other currents flowing to the summing junction. Actually, of course, it does not quite keep the input terminal at ground but at a voltage ϵ (Greek epsilon), which is equal to the output voltage divided by the gain of the amplifier. Since the output voltage is usually less than 10 volts and the amplifier gain is on the order of 100,000, ϵ is very small.

For an 8-bit DAC the current sent to the summing amplifier by the $R-2R$ network is

$$I_{in}\left(\frac{1}{2}\ B_7 + \frac{1}{4}\ B_6 + \cdots + \frac{1}{256}\ B_0\right),$$

where B_7–B_0 are the values (0 or 1) of the digital signal. This then sums up currents in a fashion similar to the ladder network we discussed earlier. It has the advantage that the output range can be adjusted by changing the size of R_s, the feedback resistor, and the further advantage that you can put two of these DACs in series, the output of the first serving as the reference voltage for the second, and when you do this, the output of the second DAC is the product of the two digital numbers driving the DACs. For this reason these are sometimes called "multiplying" DACs.

In order to have our reverberation unit capable of passing high frequencies, we must do lots of inputs and outputs per second. We will explore this in the next chapter, but right now let's take it as a given. So we must use a DAC that doesn't take all day to do its job. That implies that the time averaging DAC is out, and we have to use either a ladder or an $R-2R$ type DAC. Since a DAC, such as the ADC-MC8BC or the MC1408, costs only around $10, this is not too expensive a proposition. We will need a DAC connected to the output port we called DELAY and another connected to the output port called NORMAL.

ANALOG TO DIGITAL CONVERSION

We have seen above how to generate an analog voltage that is proportional to a digital number stored inside the computer. Now we are going to use such a DAC to help us convert an analog voltage into a digital number. What we need in addition to a DAC is a comparator (see Figure 5.11).

The unknown input voltage and the output of the DAC are compared. If the unknown is larger, we increase the output of the DAC until they are equal. Figure 5.12 shows an algorithm that will eventually find the value of the unknown voltage. This is sometimes called a "ramp" or "counter" type of converter. Such devices are available commercially with the program built into the hardware. The main problem, of course, is that it is slow, typically requiring 500 microseconds for a conversion.

A second type of A to D converter is called a "binary search" type. We start with the DAC outputting a voltage of half the maximum. If that is too small, we try 3/4; if it is too large we try 1/4. Now, depending on the outcome of the test, we add or subtract an eighth, then a sixteenth, and so forth. Figure 5.13 shows an algorithm for this kind of A to D. Chips with this algorithm wired in are available for under $10. One example is the MM5357. They typically take 25 microseconds to do an 8-bit A to D conversion. Other chips are available to give more accurate measurements of an analog voltage, and 10- and 12-bit converters are available as well as 8-bit.

As before, we are interested in speed, so we will use a binary search A to D connected to the INPUT port. Usually an A to D converter needs a signal to tell it to start the conversion, and it generates a signal when that task is finished. Assuming we have type 6520 I/O ports, we can use lines I_1 and I_2 of a type A port to do handshaking with the A to D. When we read the value from the data register, that will pulse I_2, telling the A to D to begin a conversion. Before reading a value from the data register, we should test bit C_7 of the control register to see if it has been set by I_1, meaning that the conversion is complete and the number in the data register is stable and valid.

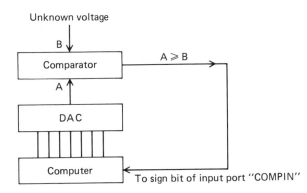

Figure 5.11 *A DAC and a comparator assembled to act as an A to D converter.*

```
BEGIN:      LDAIM     0              Load a 0.
LOOP:       STA       TEMP           Store it in TEMP.
            OUTPUT    DAC            Output the value.
            INPUT     COMPVALUE      Read the output of the comparator.
            BMA       DONE
            LDA       TEMP
            ADDIM     1
            JMP       LOOP
DONE:
```

Figure 5.12 *An algorithm for a ramp-type output to discover the value of an unknown analog signal.*

Exercise 5.1

Figures 5.14 and 5.15 show a simplified circuit for experimenting. There is a microphone and an operational amplifier to bring the amplitude of the signal up to about 1 or 2 volts RMS or a max of 5 volts, peak to peak. This feeds an A to D connected to an input port. Your delay algorithm connects the input port with the output port that drives a DAC that drives a small power amplifier and speaker.

```
BEGIN:        LDAIM     128           Start at the midpoint.
              STA       STEP          Set the step size.
LOOP:         STA       TEMP          Set the size of the DAC output.
              OUTPUT    DAC
              INPUT     COMPVALUE     Read the state of the comparator.
              BMA       TOOBIG        DAC ≥ UNKNOWN.
TOO SMALL:    LDA       STEP
              ASR                     Divide step size by 2.
              BZA       DONE          If step size is down to 0, exit.
              STA       STEP
              ADD       TEMP
              JMP       LOOP          Try with a larger value.
TOO BIG:      LDA       STEP
              ASR
              BZA       DONE
              STA       STEP          Divide step size by 2.
              LDA       TEMP
              SUB       STEP
              JMP       LOOP          Try a smaller value.
DONE:
```

Figure 5.13 *A binary search algorithm for analog to digital conversion.*

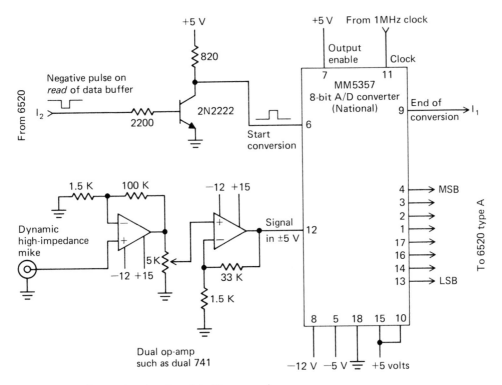

Figure 5.14 *Input circuitry for A to D conversion.*

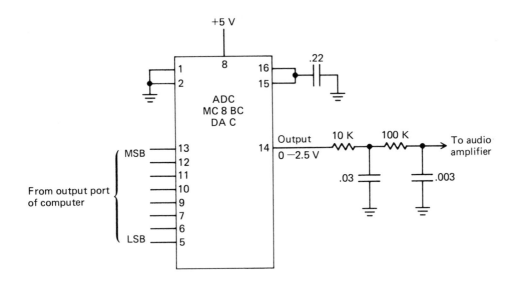

Figure 5.15 *Output circuits for D to A conversion.*

For starters, make the program be a plain delay with no reverberation. When everything is working satisfactorily, flick the microphone with a fingernail. You should hear a tick and then a fraction of a second later a simple tick coming out of the speaker. Now bring the microphone closer to the speaker until when you flick the mike once, you get a train of pulses dying out over time. You are adding reverberation by feeding back the output into the input. If you add too much, the net gain will be larger than one, and the system will begin to howl in typical feedback fashion.

Replace your straight delay algorithm with one that retains 15/16 of the old signal (see Figure 5.5), and observe the same train of dying echoes, even when the mike and speaker are far apart.

6 The Sampling Theorem

In this chapter we are going to investigate how many samples we need to take per second of a signal in order to be sure of being able to reproduce that signal again. Not to drag out the suspense past the breaking point, the answer is "at least two samples per period of the signal." That answer can be reached by moderately complicated mathematical procedures. If you want to see that sort of approach, you have come to the wrong book. Here we are going to present to you what is

---

WHY STUDY SAMPLED DATA SYSTEMS?

When computers are used to observe the world around them, the best they can do is to take occasional "snapshots" of the world called "samples." If a computer does nothing but "input, input, input," it wouldn't have time to do any computing based on that input, and even in this case it could read the number in the input port only once every five microseconds or so.

If the world is changing slowly and the computer sampling rapidly, then it is obvious that the computer can find out all there is to know about the world from its samples and perhaps by interpolating values between samples if necessary. But suppose that just after the computer has taken a sample, some brief transient event occurs in the world outside, and that by the time the next sample is taken all traces of the event have disappeared. Then the computer would have missed that event entirely.

A more complicated and potentially more dangerous situation can arise because of the stroboscopic effect of taking samples. A phenomenon that is actually taking place at one rate can appear to be happening at another rate. This is called "aliasing." If one intends to use a computer to control some aspect of the real world, one had better know when such behavior might occur and what to do about it if it does. For this reason we are going to look at some aspects of sampled data systems.

disparagingly called a "heuristic argument." That's one in which if you don't look at it too closely, it seems okay, but which offers no guarantee that there are not terrible flaws down inside that could blow the whole thing apart just at the wrong moment. Stated another way, a heuristic argument might possibly help you to understand something, but don't try to use it to convince your theoretical friends (if any).

We are going to assume that instead of an inexpensive microcomputer, we have a machine more powerful than any dreamt of in the halls of IBM or CDC. This tame giant is going to be able to compute arbitrarily complex functions in no time at all. It will be able to measure with infinite precision, and it will be able to change its output signal by as small an amount as may be desired at least once very nanosecond. Our one single restriction on this computational behemoth is that it can catch a glimpse of the input signal only once each millisecond.

Being kind as well as wise and good magicians, we are going to let our colossus take as many samples of the input signal as it wishes. And what incredible task are we going to set for this mighty engine? Why, simply to reproduce the input signal—a job that could be accomplished superbly well by a short length of copper wire connecting the input terminals directly to the output terminals.

STROBOSCOPIC STOP ACTION

We have all seen westerns in which the bandits were pursuing the stagecoach that was rushing along at great speed, rocking from side to side in imminent danger of capsizing, and then we noticed that the wheels were turning only very slowly or, indeed, turning backward. That is not due to a failure of the special effects department to keep the wheels of the "propped up" stagecoach moving at the right rate. It is a phenomenon known as stroboscopic stop action. The movie camera opens its shutter 24 times a second and takes a sample (a snapshot) of the universe before it. These regularly spaced samples are projected on a screen, and the computer behind our eyes connects them up to give the appearance of motion. If the wheels of the stagecoach have N spokes and during the 24th of a second between frames the wheel turns just $1/N$ revolution, there are spokes in exactly the same places there were when the last frame was exposed, and we see the wheel standing still. If it has turned slightly more than $1/N$ revolution, we see the wheel moving slowly in the forward direction; slightly less, and we see it turning slowly backward. Because we know the stagecoach is moving forward and the wheels are in contact with the ground, we know that they must *really* be turning forward. We know this from other clues, not from the pictures of the wheels, and without those external clues we would be unable to determine, from the picture of the wheel alone, whether it was really stopped or really turning. Now let's see how this can happen with electrical signals and computers.

ANOTHER WAY TO LOOK AT IT

Imagine that we have a white disk with a black dot on it, turned by a variable-speed motor. Let a stroboscope flash a bright light on the disk once a second for a very short interval of time—say, 1 microsecond (see Figure 6.1). Now start the motor turning the disk counterclockwise at 10° per second, or 36 seconds per revolution or complete cycle. We see the dot on the disk assuming successive positions of 10, 20, 30, . . . degrees. If the motor were turning clockwise, we would see angles of 0°, 350°, 340°, and so forth. Now for a moment let us forget the strobe light, and allow me to convince you that in the world we are interested in, the world of sine waves, there is no real difference between turning clockwise and turning counterclockwise. A sine wave is basically one-dimensional, so let us measure the projection of the dot on the Y axis rather than its position in two-dimensional space. The projection will rise and fall along the Y axis in a sinusoidal wave, exactly the same whether the disk is turning clockwise or counterclockwise (see Figure 6.2). There will be a difference in phase, depending on the direction and initial position, but the same sine wave will be traced out in either case.

Back to the strobe light. The motor turns faster, and now it is seen at positions of 0, 20, 40, 60, . . . degrees. Faster yet, and we see it at 0, 90, 180, 270, and 0 again. Still faster, let us assume that the disk is turning 170° per second counterclockwise. Now we see the dot at 0°, 170°, 340°, 150°, and so on, as in Figure 6.3. If the motor turns just a bit faster, we will see the bar at exactly 0° and 180° and at no other spots. But suppose instead the disk was turning clockwise and turning 190° per second. The picture we see of successive dot positions is identical to that shown in Figure 6.3. We would see 0°, 170°, 340°, 150°, . . . , and so on. We can't tell the difference between 170° per second counterclockwise and 190° per second clockwise. By symmetry, of course, we couldn't tell the difference between 170° per second clockwise and 190° per second counterclockwise. But from the previous argument we can't tell the difference between clockwise and counterclockwise, so a speed of 170° per second will look the same as a speed of 190° per second.

Now suppose the disk turns 170 + 360 = 530 degrees per second. It still looks like 170° or 190°. If it turns 170 + N * 360 degrees per second, we get the same answer.

So 180° per second (or one half a revolution per second) (or one half the frequency of the strobe light) is a magic quantity, and frequencies a little bit below half a cycle per second and a little bit above half a cycle per second look identical, as will frequencies either side of 3/2 cycles per second and 5/2 and so forth.

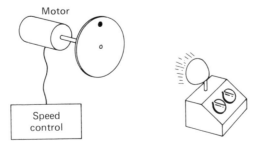

Figure 6.1 *Variable-speed motor, disk, and stroboscope.*

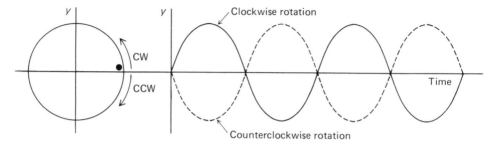

Figure 6.2 *A rotating disk and the projection of the dot onto the y axis.*

Now consider a disk turning 370° per second. With a strobe light flashing once per second, we couldn't tell that disk from one turning 10° per second or even one turning 350° per second. In summary, then, we have "folding" frequencies at all half multiples of *F*—the frequency of the strobe light (of the sampler). At even half multiples (at *F*, 2*F*, 3*F*, etc.),. the apparent frequencies are small (near zero degrees per second) while near odd half multiples the apparent frequencies are as high as we can ever observe—close to 180° per time-period-between-flashes. Half the frequency of the strobe is called the Nyquist frequency, and Figure 6.4 shows the apparent frequency as a function of the real frequency and the sampling frequency, *F*.

SAMPLING A SINE WAVE

Figure 6.5 shows some sine waves and samples taken of their magnitudes at regular intervals. We choose to take samples every four time units, and we show frequencies of 1/18, 1/14, 1/12, and 1/10. Each shows a different pattern, and it is possible to believe that with our supercomputer working very fast, we could reconstitute the original sine waves. Actually, all that is needed is a low pass filter, but let that pass and let the supercomputer do its job.

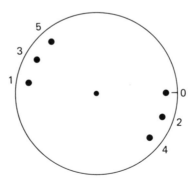

Figure 6.3 *The disk is turning 170° per second counterclockwise. Successive illuminations are numbered 0,1,....*

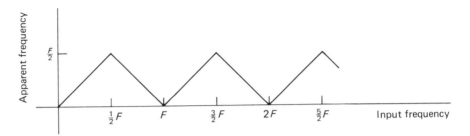

Figure 6.4 *The apparent frequency as a function of the input frequency. The sampler is taking F samples per second.*

Now look at Figure 6.6. We show frequencies of 1/10 and 3/20 sampled at a period of four. We show them first separately and then superimposed. Two different frequencies have generated the same pattern of samples. A note on construction of the figure. We used 1/4 inch quadrille graph paper. The samples were taken every four squares, or once per inch. The lower-frequency (longer-period) sine was chosen to have a period of 10 divisions; the higher-frequency sine had a period of 6⅔ divisions. The frequency of a signal is equal to one over its period, and the "Nyquist period" is considered to be twice the time separation between a pair of samples, eight divisions in this case.

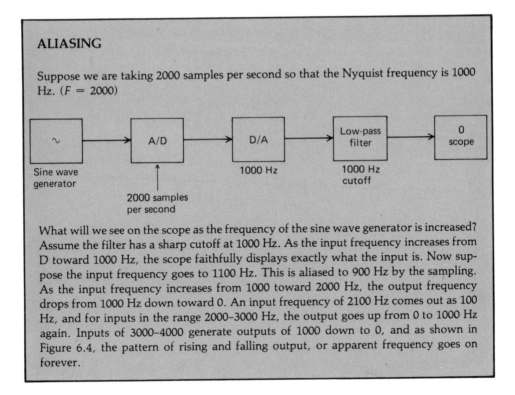

ALIASING

Suppose we are taking 2000 samples per second so that the Nyquist frequency is 1000 Hz. $(F = 2000)$

What will we see on the scope as the frequency of the sine wave generator is increased? Assume the filter has a sharp cutoff at 1000 Hz. As the input frequency increases from D toward 1000 Hz, the scope faithfully displays exactly what the input is. Now suppose the input frequency goes to 1100 Hz. This is aliased to 900 Hz by the sampling. As the input frequency increases from 1000 toward 2000 Hz, the output frequency drops from 1000 Hz down toward 0. An input frequency of 2100 Hz comes out as 100 Hz, and for inputs in the range 2000–3000 Hz, the output goes up from 0 to 1000 Hz again. Inputs of 3000–4000 generate outputs of 1000 down to 0, and as shown in Figure 6.4, the pattern of rising and falling output, or apparent frequency goes on forever.

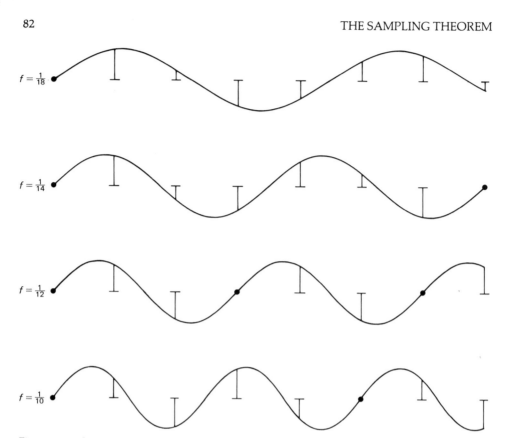

Figure 6.5   *Some sine waves with samples of their magnitudes.*

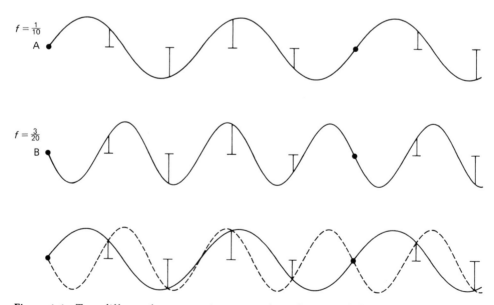

Figure 6.6   *Two different frequency sine waves that when sampled appear to be identical.*

So $f_1 = 1/10$ is the frequency of the lower note, and $f_0 = 1/8$ is the Nyquist frequency. We choose f_2 such that

$$f_2 = f_0 + (f_0 - f_1)$$

or

$$f_2 = 1/8 + 1/8 - 1/10 = 3/20.$$

This gives a period of $6\frac{2}{3}$ divisions.

First we drew the lower-frequency curve and then selected an arbitrary starting point for the first sample. Other samples were thus fixed to follow every fourth division. The curve of the higher frequency was drawn on transparent paper and slid along the figure until the points over the sampling instants had the same values as the lower-frequency curve. Is this cheating? No. All we did was to show that for an arbitrary frequency (f_1) and sampling period we could find a phase relationship (sliding position) for a curve of frequency f_2 that, when sampled, would look just like f_1. So if both f_1 and f_2 exist in my signal, how can I tell them apart with a sampling period of $1/2f_0$? The answer is I can't, so I had better be sure that *both* f_1 and f_2 are not present.

The way this is generally stated is sort of backward to the above, but it comes out the same. It is called the "fundamental sampling theorem" and says:

> "If the highest frequency *present* in the input signal is f, then in order to be able to reconstruct that signal, you must take at least $2f$ samples per second."

This is absolutely true, but what many people do is rephrase it to say:

> "If the highest frequency *of interest* in the input . . . ,"

which is false. Let us prove that empirically.

Exercise 6.1

The following brief program will sample the input approximately once every millisecond.

LOOP:	INPUT	PORT A	Sample input and
	OUTPUT	PORT B	shove it out other side.
	LDAIM	200	Put decimal 200 in the accumulator.
DELAY:	SUBIM	1	Count down in
	BNA	DELAY	5-microsecond loop.
	JMP	LOOP	Repeat.

Connect the computer as shown in Figure 6.7. Details of the A/D and D/A converters are shown in Figures 5.13 and 5.14. If you sample once per millisecond, your Nyquist frequency will be 500 Hz. With the amplifier connected to the output

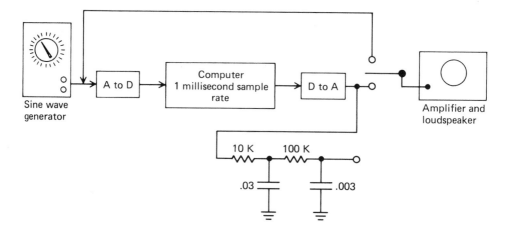

Figure 6.7   *Test setup for experiments on digital filters.*

of the computer, vary the input frequency until you get two tones that sound the same. The sampling process will introduce a good bit of high-frequency noise into the signal, so it would be wise to add a two-stage RC filter on the output of the DAC, as shown in Figure 4.3. You can purchase a fine DAC with a 6-pole (very sharp cutoff) filter for about $50 from Micro Technology Unlimited, all made up neatly on a small card that can be driven by any 8-bit output port.

With this setup, 400 hertz and 600 hertz will sound identical if the Nyquist frequency really is 500 hertz. The 600-Hz signal is said to be "aliasing" as a 400-Hz signal. To prove that nobody is cheating, connect the amplifier to the output of the oscillator, and verify that 400 and 600 are *not* the same before computer processing. Look for other "mirrored" pairs. You should find equivalences like these:

$$100 \text{ Hz} = 900 \text{ Hz}$$
$$200 \text{ Hz} = 800 \text{ Hz}$$
$$300 \text{ Hz} = 700 \text{ Hz}$$
$$400 \text{ Hz} = 600 \text{ Hz}$$
$$450 \text{ Hz} = 550 \text{ Hz}$$
etc.

Of course, these numbers will be balanced on either side of some other mirror or Nyquist frequency if the initial count put in the accumulator is different. Change that count to 150 decimal in the above code, and by measurements such as those above discover the new Nyquist frequency.

Now go back to a Nyquist frequency of 500 hertz. What happens if we put a signal in the range between 1000 Hz and 1500 Hz? How about the range from 1500 to 2000? From 2000 to 2500? Explain this phenomenom with reference to a picture like Figure 6.4.

NONSINUSOIDAL INPUTS

So far we have considered only sinusoidal inputs and presented an argument that sine waves of all frequencies from 0 up to f_0 can be captured and reproduced from samples taken every $1/2f_0$ seconds. What about nonsine waves? Things like square waves or triangular waves or complex wave shapes, such as those produced by a clarinet? Certainly we can't investigate each and every possible wave shape to see if it will pass through the sampler, nor do we need to, for there is a simpler way. A mathematical theorem by a Frenchman named Fourier saves the day. It says, in effect, that any repetitive wave form may be viewed as being made up of a collection of sine waves, and further, with a sufficiently warped mind any signal is repetitive.

Then as long as the frequency of the highest-frequency sine wave making up a signal is below the Nyquist frequency, we can sample the input signal and later reconstitute it, just like orange juice, from the samples alone. What happens if there *are* frequencies in the input that exceed the mirror frequency? If we let them through to the sampler, it would get confused and treat these high frequencies as if they were their aliases and so confuse the whole process of reproduction. To keep these evil frequencies away from our poor sensitive sampler, we are going to use a low pass filter, and to find out all about that, read the next chapter.

7 Filters, Digital and Otherwise

There is an old story about an audiophile walking out of a symphony shaking his head sadly and muttering "Not enough bass. Not enough bass." In this chapter we may not be able to put you more in touch with the real world than that audiophile, but we will tell you what a filter is and how it can be used to eliminate undesired sounds—or increase the bass if that is what you want.

A LOW-PASS FILTER

The outside world gets moderately unpleasant. Bad weather appears, let us say. People rush into a safe room through its narrow door. The first through the narrow door see an empty room and are glad to come in. The next ones along find a partially filled room and enter more slowly. Soon the room is crowded with people, and more enter only reluctantly until at last it is so crowded that those outside would just as soon face the bad weather as the sardinelike conditions inside the room, and no more come through the door. When an hour later the storm goes away, the people stream out, fast at first (with great relief) and then more slowly as there becomes room to breathe. Figure 7.1 shows the weather of the outside world and the count of the number of people per square foot in the room. As long as the time between appearances and disappearances of storms is sufficiently long, the room will empty and fill completely, but suppose we have a periodic storm that comes and goes every five minutes when the room is only partially filled or emptied. Clearly the larger the room, the more people it will take to fill it, and the longer, too. The more restrictive the doorway, the longer it will take.

Let us replace the doorway with a resistor R, the room with a capacitor C, the storm with an external source of voltage V, and instead of people per square foot, we will talk of the voltage across the capacitor: V_c. Figure 7.2 shows the electrical circuit we have been discussing. This is called a "low-pass filter" because it passes low frequencies but not high frequencies. If we multiply R in ohms times C in

WHY STUDY DIGITAL FILTERS?

Suppose that you believed that if you could only get rid of the day-to-day fluctuations and look at the long-term trends, you would be able to tell whether a stock was going up or down. Or perhaps you would like to prove that it really does rain just on weekends, and that there is a seven-day cycle in the weather. Or maybe you have some "wow" on the tape that you would like to remove from an irreplaceable live recording of Nemo and the Captains playing "Underwater Delights." In each of these cases you would be interested in filtering out parts of the signal and emphasizing other parts.

Analog filters have been around for many years in many forms. Recently attention has turned to digital filters for several reasons:

1. Once a program is working properly, it can be reproduced at will. There is no worry about component tolerances and alignment, such as must be done for analog filters.

2. Size, weight, and expense are often on the side of the digital filter.

3. With digital filters it is possible to do things that are completely impractical to achieve with analog filters.

farads, we get something called the RC time constant. Let us take an RC time constant of 1, for example, by having $R = 1$ million ohms and $C = 1$ microfarad. We begin with a very low frequency voltage V, with $f = 0.001$ cycles per second. The capacitor has plenty of time to fill and empty and therefore has almost no effect, and $V_2 \simeq V_1$. Now we choose a high frequency of 1000 cycles per second. The

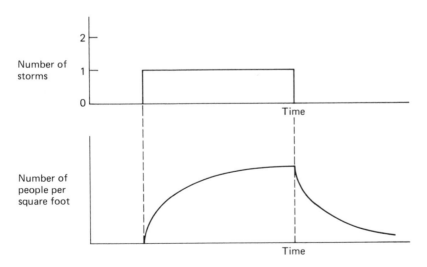

Figure 7.1 *Population density as a function of time.*

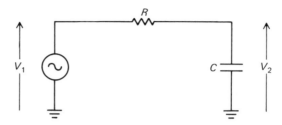

Figure 7.2 *An RC low-pass filter.*

variations in the input are so rapid the capacitor is unable to follow the signal at all, and for all intents and purposes $V_2=0$. How about the midrange around 1 cycle per second? Figure 7.3 shows the amplitude of the signal V_2 as a function of the frequency of the input signal. For reasons we don't need to labor over here (see any good introduction to AC circuits), when the frequency f is given by

$$f = \frac{1}{2\pi\,RC} \ ,$$

then V_2 will be .707 of the amplitude of V_1. The moral of all this is that low frequencies get through and high frequencies do not.

An "ideal" low-pass filter (which, unfortunately, we are not able to obtain) would have a frequency response like that of Figure 7.4.

Another way to characterize a low-pass filter is to ask how long the output takes to fall to some standard fraction of its initial value after the input is set to zero. The fraction usually chosen is $1/e$ where e is 2.718, the base of the natural logarithms. For an RC filter this time turns out to be just the RC time constant.

Now let us ask how we might reproduce such a low-pass filter using only a computer program. Consider the setup of Figure 7.5. The input is X and the output is Y. The computer is set up to calculate the following functions:

$$Y_k = BX_k + AY_{k-1} \ .$$

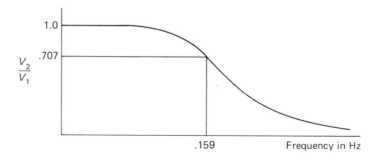

Figure 7.3 *The frequency response of an RC low-pass filter.*

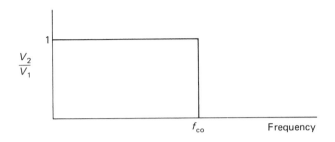

Figure 7.4 *An ideal low-pass filter; f_{co} is the "cutoff" frequency.*

RC FILTERS

If we plot the gain of a simple low-pass *RC* filter versus the input frequency on log-log paper (that is, we plot the logarithm of the gain against the logarithm of the frequency), we get a curve that looks like the dotted line in the sketch.

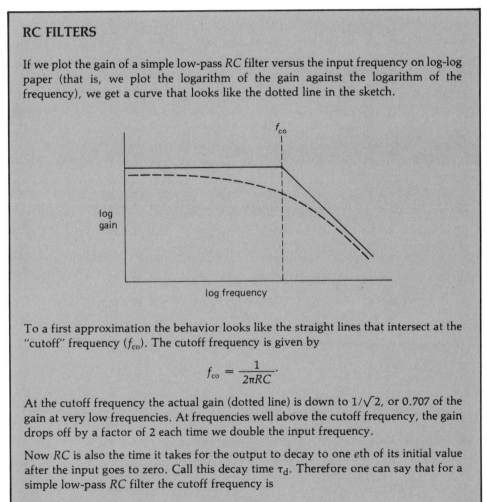

To a first approximation the behavior looks like the straight lines that intersect at the "cutoff" frequency (f_{co}). The cutoff frequency is given by

$$f_{co} = \frac{1}{2\pi RC}.$$

At the cutoff frequency the actual gain (dotted line) is down to $1/\sqrt{2}$, or 0.707 of the gain at very low frequencies. At frequencies well above the cutoff frequency, the gain drops off by a factor of 2 each time we double the input frequency.

Now *RC* is also the time it takes for the output to decay to one *e*th of its initial value after the input goes to zero. Call this decay time τ_d. Therefore one can say that for a simple low-pass *RC* filter the cutoff frequency is

$$f_{co} = \frac{1}{2\pi \cdot \tau_d}.$$

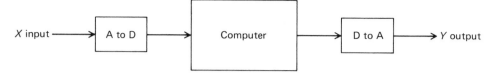

Figure 7.5 *Setup for a typical digital filter. For details see Figures 5.13 and 5.14.*

That is, the new value for the output is the linear sum of the old output and the current input. We want the filter to have unity gain at DC (or zero frequency) input, so when $X_k = 1$ for a very long time, we want

$$Y_k = Y_{k-1} = 1 .$$

To satisfy this, we require that

$$A + B = 1 .$$

What we have written here can be translated into words with no great difficulty:

"We are going to take a large number of samples of the input:

$$X_1, X_2, X_3, X_4, \ldots , X_k, \ldots$$

and so on. Each time we take an input sample, we compute a new value for the output. This new value is a function of both the present input and the old (previous) value of the output."

Let us see what happens if the input is held at one for a very long time and then is allowed to go to zero. Assume values for A and B such that

$$Y_k = 1/8 \, X_k + 7/8 \, Y_{k-1} .$$

We will construct a table to calculate Y_k. Assume that the input goes to zero when $k = 1$.

k	input	old output	new output
-100	1	1	1
-1	1	1	1
0	1	1	1
1	0		
2	0		
3	0		
4	0		

This much we can construct from the statement of the problem. Now consider the line $k = 1$. The old value of the output (when $k = 0$) is known to be 1, so we can write

k	input	old output	new output
1	0	1	?

The new output will be

$$\frac{1}{8} \cdot 0 + \frac{7}{8} \cdot 1 = \frac{7}{8} \cdot$$

For the next line we have

k	input	old output	new output
2	0	$\frac{7}{8}$	?

and we can calculate that

$$Y_2 = \frac{1}{8} \cdot 0 + \frac{7}{8} \cdot \frac{7}{8} = .76 \cdot$$

Again

$$Y_3 = \frac{1}{8} \cdot 0 + \frac{7}{8} \cdot Y_2 = \frac{7}{8} \times .76 = .67 \cdot$$

We can fill out the rest of the table as far into the future as we like. Summarizing we have:

k	Y_k	k	Y_k
0	1.0	6	.45
1	.875	7	.39
2	.76	8	.34
3	.67	9	.30
4	.59	10	.26
5	.51		

We can also plot this function as in Figure 7.6. Notice carefully that we haven't yet said anything about "time" or about "how fast" the output will decay to 1/eth of its initial value. Since $1/e \sim .368$, we know already from looking at the table just above that we will be down to 1/eth of the input by the eighth sample, but we don't know *when* that will be until we specify how many samples we are going to take per minute. If we are taking one sample per week, then after 8 weeks the signal is down to 1/eth of its initial value. If we are taking 1 sample per microsecond, then it is down in 8 microseconds.

Table 7.1 shows the rate of decay of several filters that are easy to program without a hardware multiplier. We have underlined the first value in each column that is less than or equal to 1/e. It seems that our low-pass digital filter will be down to 1/eth of an initial value after $1/B$ samples, or if T is the time between

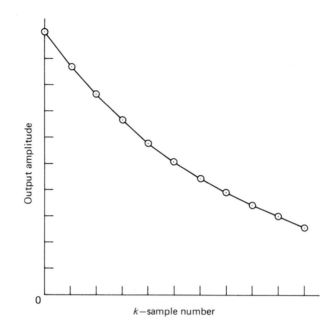

Figure 7.6 *A plot of the values calculated for the digital filter.*

samples, then after T/B seconds. This corresponds to the RC time constant of our analog filter. By analogy, the "cutoff" frequency of this filter would be

$$f = \frac{B}{2\pi T}.$$

For example, with 50 microseconds between samples (20,000 SPS) and a B of 1/16, we find

$$f = \frac{1/16}{2\pi 50 \times 10^{-6}} = 198.9 \text{ hertz.}$$

Figure 7.7 shows a plot of the frequency at which the gain is down to .707 of the low-frequency gain as a function of B. Frequency is shown as a fraction of the Nyquist frequency. Thus for $B = .5$ and a Nyquist frequency of 10,000 Hz (50 microseconds between samples), the gain would be down to .707 at 2300 Hz. For $B = .25$ the gain is down to .707 at 900 Hz (assuming a 10K Hz Nyquist frequency).

The solid curve is the correct theoretical value predicted by sampling theory. The circled crosses represent our predicted cutoff frequency based on the analogy with analog filters. As may be seen, this is not a bad rule of thumb for values of B less than 1/4, but it is somewhat lacking for values larger than that.

Figure 7.8 shows the gain versus frequency curves for several values of B that are easy to compute. Once again we plot the gain normalized to unity at 0 frequency and the frequency as a fraction of the Nyquist frequency.

Table 7.1 Rates of Decay of a Low-Pass Digital Filter, where $Y_k = BX_k + AY_{k-1}$

k	$A = 1/2$	$A = 3/4$	$A = 7/8$	$A = 15/16$	$A = 31/32$
0	1	1	1	1	1
1	.500	.750	.875	.937	.969
2	.250	.562	.766	.879	.938
3	.125	.422	.670	.824	.909
4	.062	.316	.586	.772	.881
5	.031	.237	.513	.724	.853
6	.016	.178	.449	.679	.827
7	.008	.133	.393	.637	.801
8	.004	.100	.344	.597	.776
9	.002	.075	.301	.559	.751
10	.001	.056	.263	.524	.728
11				.492	.705
12				.461	.683
13				.432	.662
14				.405	.641
15				.380	.621
16				.356	.602
17					.583
18					.565
19					.547
20					.530
21					.513
22					.497
23					.482
24					.467
25					.452
26					.438
27					.424
28					.411
29					.398
30					.386
31					.374
32					.362

Exercise 7.1

Set up the microcomputer as indicated in Figure 7.5 with an audio oscillator connected to X. Write a program that will compute

$$Y_k = \frac{1}{16} X_k + \frac{15}{16} Y_{k-1}$$

and take samples every 50 microseconds similar to:

```
LOOP:   INPUT      PORTA     ⎫
        ARS                  ⎪
        ARS                  ⎬   Divide input by 16 and save it at
        ARS                  ⎪              NEWVALUE.
        ARS                  ⎪
        STA        NEWVALUE  ⎭
        LDA        OLDVALUE  ⎫
        ARS                  ⎪
        ARS                  ⎪
        ARS                  ⎬   Take old value and divide it by
        ARS                  ⎪           16 = Y/16.
        STA        TEMP      ⎭
        LDA        OLDVALUE
        SUB        TEMP          Form 15/16 of Y.
        ADD        NEWVALUE      Add in X/16.
        STA        OLDVALUE
        OUTPUT     PORTB
        NOP                      Waste a
        NOP                      little time.
        JMP        LOOP          Do it again.
```

and run a frequency response curve for this filter. It should look a lot like Figure 7.8. A standard voltmeter (20,000 ohms/volt) will do for measuring the voltage, but an oscilloscope is better if you have one handy. Make sure the amplitude of the input signal is in the right range so that the peak values of X and Y fall between full scale and 3/4 of full scale. For example, if you are using a signed binary A to D converter, then 1 volt RMS (as measured with a volt-ohm-meter) will mean positive and negative peaks of 1.4 volts or a range of 2.8 volts. Switch the same voltmeter back and forth between input and output. That way you don't need to worry about the full-scale accuracy of the meter. Select a frequency, and adjust the source level to some standard value. Then measure the output. Assume we don't know the cutoff frequency. What frequencies should be tried? Begin with a frequency that is low enough so that you are relatively certain that you are well below the cutoff frequency. Start at, say, 10 cycles per second (properly called 10 hertz, or abbreviated as 10 Hz). Measure the gain of the system. Gain is defined as the amplitude of the output divided by the amplitude of the input. Now, without changing anything else, reduce the amplitude of the input signal to one half its previous value. Did the amplitude of the output decrease by half? if not, you are overdriving the system with too large a signal. Reduce the input signal until, when you cut it in half, the output goes down by half. Once you are in the linear range, use as large an amplitude as is convenient, since this will allow more accurate measurements. Repeat these checks at several other frequencies as you go along to make sure you are always measuring signals in the linear range.

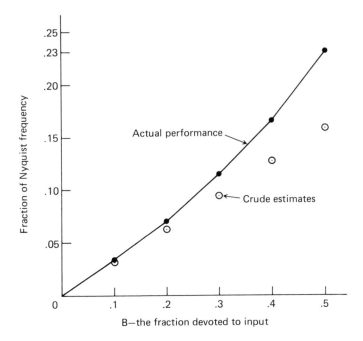

Figure 7.7 *Plot of the frequency at which the gain is reduced to .707 of the low-frequency gain as a function of B for a low-pass filter.*

Increase the frequency by a factor of 10. If the gain has not changed by more than a few percent, go up another decade in frequency. Sooner or later you will pass the cutoff frequency, and the gain will rapidly fall toward zero. Keep on increasing frequency by factors of 10 until you get up to the Nyquist frequency (in this case 10,000 Hz). Using this strategy, we would measure the gain at 10, 100, 1000, and 10,000 Hz. Most of the change of gain will appear in one decade range. Assume it is the decade between 100 Hz and 1000 Hz. Go back to that decade and measure every octave: at 100, 200, 400, 800 Hz. Find the octave in which the gain is around .75 of the low-frequency gain. Within that octave take measurements every 10% of the octave (say 200, 220, 240, etc.) until you find the points that straddle a gain of .707 (that is, the lower frequency gives a gain greater than this and the higher a gain less than this). If you have been able to keep the input at 1 volt RMS, then you can measure the gain as the output amplitude without any calculation at all. You will find that 4-cycle semilog paper is very convenient for plotting your results.

Now insert a delay in your program so that you take samples once every 100 microseconds and repeat the gain-frequency measurements. Change the algorithm so that it computes

$$Y_k = \frac{7}{8} Y_{k-1} + \frac{1}{8} X_k,$$

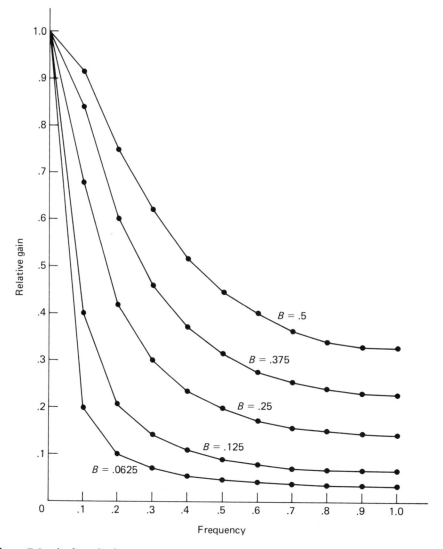

Figure 7.8 *A plot of relative gain versus frequency for several values of B.*

and measure the gain-frequency response of that filter with 50- and 100-micro-
second sampling intervals. By now you should have got the idea that changing the
sampling period merely changes the scales of the frequency; that is, 400 Hz at 50
microseconds per sample is the same (for the same equation) as 200 Hz at 100
microseconds per sample. We can form an abstract dimensionless sort of frequency
scale by plotting the ratio of the real frequency to the Nyquist frequency:

$$f^* = \frac{f}{f_n},$$

where

$$f_n = \frac{1}{2T},$$

and T = time per sample.

Replot the above results as a function of f^*.

Note: The combination of ADC and DAC chips suggested in the previous chapter will not give one volt out for one volt in. There is a change of scale in the DAC that can be corrected by an amplifier (not shown) or by measuring all gains *relative* to the gain at a very low frequency. Further, if you really want a low frequency, replace the sine wave generator by a 1.5 volt flashlight battery. That's pure DC and as low a frequency as can be found.

DOUBLE FILTERING

On the good old American theory that if a little is good a lot must be absolutely wonderful, let us low-pass filter our input signal and then low-pass filter it again to make it "more nearly ideal."

First we calculate

$$Y_k = AY_{k-1} + BX_k, \tag{7.1}$$

and then from Y we calculate

$$Z_k = AZ_{k-1} + BY_k \tag{7.2}$$

and output Z_k.

This will take about 100 microseconds to calculate for $A = 7/8$, $B = 1/8$, so plan on that. Plot the gain-frequency curve for this double filter.

We can do some mathematical manipulation of Equations 7.1 and 7.2 to get them in a different form. Taking the first equation and substituting it in the second, we get

$$Z_k = AZ_{k-1} + ABY_{k-1} + B^2 X_k. \tag{7.3}$$

Taking the second equation, rearranging, and subtracting one from the index k, we get

$$Z_{k-1} - AZ_{k-2} = BY_{k-1},$$

which we can substitute for BY_{k-1} in Equation 7.3, getting, after we collect terms,

$$Z_k = 2AZ_{k-1} - A^2 Z_{k-2} + B^2 X_k. \tag{7.4}$$

If we let a rectangle represent a unit delay and a triangle represent a multiplier, we can generalize Equation 7.4 as shown in Figure 7.9. Many very erudite books have been written about higher-order digital filters, as these are called. This book is not one of them. *An Introduction to Discrete Systems* by Kenneth Steiglitz and a book called *Digital Filters* by Richard Hamming are among the most understandable.

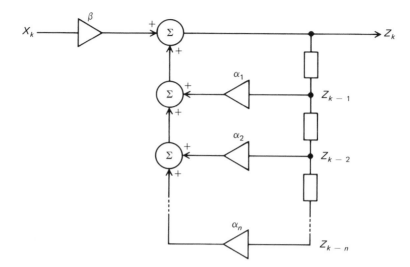

Figure 7.9 *A generalized n-stage digital filter.*

The problem with most of the books in this field is that their authors have forgotten that filters exist not for the purposes of mathematical manipulation but to filter out some signals and let others through. You would never in a million years guess that from casual reading in the field. Most of the authors lost touch with the real world so long ago they have forgotten which direction it is in. Even Steiglitz, who writes very clearly and understandably about some very complex topics, has no reference in his index for "high pass," "low pass," "band pass," or cutoff frequency, or any indication in the text that they might be of interest to some poor working slob.

HIGH-PASS FILTERS

We have spent a fair bit of time on a low-pass filter, but there are other kinds of filters of equal interest. The first of these is a high-pass filter. Consider again the basic recursive filter equation:

$$Y_k = AY_{k-1} + BX_k .$$

What we are doing is averaging the new input with the old output so that any quick, sudden changes in input will be smoothed out, leaving only the slow, long-term trends—that is, the low-frequency component. Suppose instead we declared that "if we have already seen it, we are bored by it" and want only the new and novel. From the input we will subtract and discard anything we have seen before. Mathematically,

$$Y_k = BX_k - AY_{k-1}$$

SAMPLE AND HOLD

Successive approximation or "binary search" A to D converters can behave in a peculiar fashion if the input voltage changes rapidly while the conversion is underway.

Suppose we have a 3-bit A to D and the input is changing rapidly:

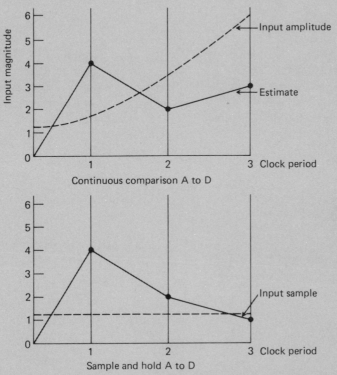

At the first clock period the device compares the input with the estimate and decides that the input is less than half the range, so it sets the first bit of the estimate to zero. At the second clock period the device decides that the input is greater than the estimate, so it makes bit 2 equal to one. At the third clock period the device again emits a one, giving an estimate of 011, or 3. But by this time the input has risen all the way to 6 on our diagram, so the answer the device comes up with does not correspond to either the input at the start of conversion or the input at the end of conversion.

The way to solve this problem is with a "sample and hold" A to D. This type of device takes a (nearly) instantaneous snapshot of the analog voltage and holds that sample constant while the conversion is taking place. In the figure above the sample would be taken at time zero and preserved. The successive approximations would follow the solid line and end with an output of one volt (001), which is a good estimate of what the input was at time zero.

represents the equation for a high-pass filter. The gain of such a high-pass filter approaches

$$G = \frac{B}{1-A}$$

as the frequency approaches the Nyquist frequency (goes as high as it can), so for no gain or loss at high frequencies, we make

$$A + B = 1 .$$

Let us assume that the input is varying as fast as an input can vary in this sampled world, namely, at the Nyquist frequency. Stating it in more ordinary terms, we assume that successive samples are alternately one and minus one. You can't change faster than that. We will assume that the world began when k changed from -1 to 0, and that Y was identically zero for negative time (time before the beginning of the world). Just to cut down on the amount of calculation, we are going to take

$$Y_k = .5X_k - .5Y_{k-1},$$

and we get:

k	X_k	Y_{k-1}	Y_k
0	1	0	.5
1	−1	.5	−.75
2	1	−.75	.875
3	−1	.875	−.9375
4	1	−.9375	.96875
5	−1	.96875	−.9844
6	1	−.9844	.9922
7	−1	.9922	−.9961
8	1	−.9961	.99805
9	−1	.99805	−.999024

Given these values of A and B, we see that Y_k very rapidly approaches X_k, which is what we would expect for a high-pass filter presented with a high-frequency signal. Calculate the values of Y_k as a function of k for the same input, and initial conditions for the filter:

$$Y_k = \frac{1}{4}X_k - \frac{3}{4}Y_{k-1} .$$

This should confirm that for $A + B = 1$ the high-frequency gain of this filter is unity. What does this filter do when the input suddenly freezes at plus one? This represents a DC or zero frequency input, and a true high-pass filter should give

---

SIGN EXTENSION FOR DIVISION

When one performs a division, one can get into trouble trying to divide negative numbers by means of right shifts. The problem is that 1100 0000, considered as a signed binary number, represents -32; but shifting the pattern right one position (which divides positive and unsigned numbers very neatly by two) gives 0110 0000, which represents $+48$, and there is no way I am going to believe that half of minus thirty-two equals forty-eight.

The way to proceed for signed numbers is to test to see if the original number is negative. If it is negative, then after the shifting is over, we can OR into the left-hand end of the word as many ones as we shifted places. For example, to divide by 8 we shift right three places. If the original number was less than zero, we should OR in the pattern 1110 0000. This has the same net effect as a shift with sign extension. Of course, if your machine has a genuine divide instruction or a sign-extending shift, you don't need to worry about this.

Using this technique to divide -32 by 2, we get:

        0110 0000   ORed with 1000 0000 (shift of one place)

giving 1110 0000, which represents -16, just what was wanted.

---

zero output. We can argue without calculating that $X_k = 1$ and $Y_k = Y_{k-1}$, so

$$Y_k = B \cdot 1 - AY_k,$$

or

$$Y_k = \frac{B}{1 + A} .$$

For $A = 7/8$, $B = 1/8$ we have a steady state value of Y of

$$Y_k = \frac{1}{15} .$$

(Come to think of it, what does our low-pass filter put out when presented with the Nyquist frequency?)

BAND-PASS FILTERS

A third class of filters that is of general interest is called a "band-pass filter." An ideal band-pass filter is shown in Figure 7.10. It passes all frequencies above f_1 and below f_2, which is consequently called the "pass band." It can be constructed by taking an ideal low-pass filter and following that with an ideal high-pass filter, or

PROGRAMMING FOR FILTERS THAT REQUIRE SUBTRACTION

Low-pass filters work out very neatly for microcomputers, because the arithmetic used does not involve subtraction, but high-pass filters and certain other more complex filters require that subtraction be performed. As soon as you allow subtraction, you have to worry about negative numbers and, hence, use signed binary.

Inexpensive A to D and D to A converters usually work with unsigned binary numbers. Thus, on input 0 volts will map to 128, and on output 128 maps to 0. To convert these numbers to use signed binary internally, it is sufficient to subtract 128 from the input and add 128 back in to convert the internal signed binary to an unsigned binary for output.

The second problem one must look out for is overflow when a signed binary number outside the range -128 to $+127$ is generated. This problem can usually be handled by decreasing the magnitude of the input signal or by doing arithmetic in double precision.

vice versa. In digital filter terms we can compute

$$Y_k = B_1X_k + A_1Y_{k-1} \tag{7.5}$$

and follow that with

$$Z_k = B_2Y_k - A_2Z_{k-1}. \tag{7.6}$$

By the same mathematical tricks we used before, we can get

$$Z_k = B_1B_2X_k + (A_1 - A_2)Z_{k-1} + A_1A_2Z_{k-2}. \tag{7.7}$$

Exercise 7.2

Write a program that will act as a band-pass filter, with the high-pass filter coefficients being

$$A_2 = 15/16,$$
$$B_2 = 1/16,$$

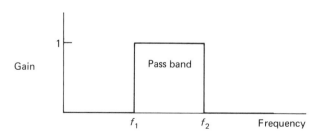

Figure 7.10 *An ideal band-pass filter.*

and the low-pass being

$$A_1 = 7/8,$$
$$B_1 = 1/8.$$

Measure the gain versus frequency for this filter. If we let $A_1 = A_2$ and $B_1 = B_2$, we get a narrow pass-band filter whose equation is

$$Z_k = B^2 X_k + A^2 Z_{k-2} .$$

Measure that filter's response curve for $A = 7/8$, $B = 1/8$.

Note: If you are going to try this experiment, you must have an A to D converter of the "sample and hold" type or else make the sampling period very long with respect to the conversion time of the ADC. Otherwise the input value will change while you are trying to measure it, with resulting confusion in the circuits.

IMPULSE RESPONSE

There is another way to characterize digital filters. It is by their response to a unit impulse on the input. That is, we assume the input is zero everywhere except when $k = 0$, at which time it is one. Given the recurrence equations we have been playing with, the impulse response is easy if tedious to calculate. Take the low-pass filter

$$Y_k = \frac{1}{8} X_k + \frac{7}{8} Y_{k-1} .$$

We construct a table similar to the ones we have done before, as follows:

k	X_k	old Y	new Y
-10	0	0	0
-1	0	0	0
0	1	0	.125
1	0	.125	.109
2	0	.109	.096
3	0	.096	.084
4	0	.084	.073
5	0	.073	.064
6	0	.064	.056
7	0	.056	.049
8	0	.049	.043
9	0	.043	.038
10	0	.038	.033

For a high-pass filter we have

$$Y_k = \frac{1}{8} X_k - \frac{7}{8} Y_{k-1} ,$$

which looks the same as the above, except that the signs alternate plus and minus

k	X_k	new Y
0	1	$+.125$
1	0	$-.109$
2	0	$+.096$
3	0	$-.084$
etc.		

So far, I note that you have managed to restrain your wild enthusiasm over this information, but wait till you find out this next bit. If the impulse at $k=0$ were of size S_k instead of 1, all the responses would be scaled up by a factor of S_k. Any set of samples of arbitrary magnitudes can be viewed as a set of impulses of those magnitudes, and the response of the filter can be calculated by adding up the response to the first impulse plus the response to the second impulse plus the . . . right on down to the end of time. We can therefore calculate the response of any linear recursive digital filter to an arbitrary input.

Take the filter

$$Y_k = \frac{1}{2}X_k + \frac{1}{2}Y_{k-1}$$

and subject it to a triangular input signal that goes: 0, 1, 2, 3, 4, 3, 2, 1, 0, 1, 2, 3, ...

First off, the impulse response of the filter is

k	X_k	Y_k
0	1	.5
1	0	.25
2	0	.125
3	0	.063
4	0	.031
5	0	.016
6	0	.008

if we stop when we get down to fractions contributing less than 1% to the output. Now consider the impulse at time k. Suppose it is of size 3; then this will contribute 1.5 units to the output at time k and .75 at time $k + 1$ and .375 at time $k + 2$ and so on. The impulse of 2 at $k = 2$ contributes 1 at $k = 2$, .5 at $k = 3$, .25 at $k = 4$, etc. Each sample contributes a column trailing off into the future as the effect of that sample dies out. Adding up all the contributions at a given time produces the net output at that instant. At $k = 2$ we get .25 from the old input plus .5 times 2, or 1, from the present input. Table 7.2 shows the calculations carried out for the first twelve samples, and Figure 7.11 shows a plot of the output over the same period. Notice that, as you might expect, the sudden changes at the corners of the triangular wave form have been smoothed off, and the output is slightly delayed with respect to the input.

Table 7.2 Calculation of Response of Low-Pass Filter to Triangular Input.

k	X_k	Contributions to the Output	
0	0		= 0
1	1	.5	= .5
2	2	.25 + 1	= 1.25
3	3	.125 + .5 + 1.5	= 2.125
4	4	.063 + .25 + .75 + 2.0	= 3.06
5	3	.031 + .125 + .375 + 1.0 + 1.5	= 3.03
6	2	.016 + .063 + .188 + .5 + .75 + 1	= 2.52
7	1	.008 + .031 + .094 + .25 + .375 + .5 + .5	= 1.76
8	0	.016 + .047 + .125 + .188 + .25 + .25 + 0	= .88
9	1	.008 + .023 + .063 + .094 + .125 + .125 + 0 + .5	= .94
10	2	.012 + .031 + .047 + .063 + .063 + 0 + .25 + 1.0	= 1.47
11	3	.006 + .016 + .023 + .031 + .031 + 0 + .125 + .5 + 1.5	= 2.23
12	4	.008 + .012 + .016 + .016 + 0 + .063 + .25 + .75 + 2	= 3.12
13	3	.006 + .008 + .008 + 0 + .031 + .125 + .375 + 1	
14	2	.004 + .004 + 0 + .016 + .063 + .188 + .5	
15	1	.008 + 0 + .031 + .094 + .25	
16	0	.016 + .047 + .125	
		.006 + .023 + .063	
		.012 + .031	
		.006 + .016	

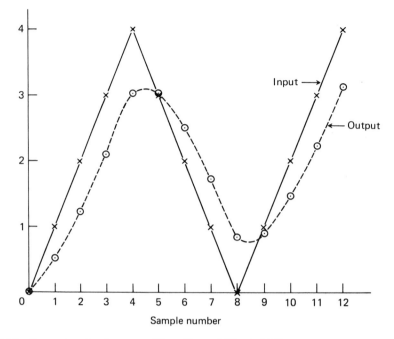

Figure 7.11 *Response of a low-pass filter, $Y_k = \frac{1}{2}X_k + \frac{1}{2}Y_{k-1}$.*

Given an input that is 0, 0, 0, 1, 1, 1, 0, 0, 0, 1, 1, 1, ..., etc., calculate and plot the response of a band-pass filter for which

$$Z_k = \frac{1}{64} X_k + \frac{49}{64} Z_{k-2}.$$

8 Closing the Loop

One of the great achievements of James Watt (1736–1819) was the improvement of the steam engine to act on the expansion pressure of the steam rather than on the vacuum left when the steam condensed. His most important invention, however, was the development and application of the governor for the steam engine. It was desired to keep a shaft turning at a constant rate, despite fluctuations in load and in the supply of steam. What he did was to measure the rate of turning of the shaft by using a fly ball governor (see Figure 8.1). As the shaft went faster, the balls flew out due to centrifugal force and, in so doing, pulled up a lever that decreased the supply of steam to the engine, thus slowing the engine down. As the shaft turned slower, the balls fell in toward their support, pushing the lever down, opening up the steam supply, and hence speeding up the engine. Notice particularly that the governor simply measured the speed of the engine. It then applied that information to control a source of energy that drove the engine.

Another early example of a complex machine is a windmill. We have all seen a farm windmill with a number of blades set in a circle and a vane sticking out behind. The wind striking the vane turns the head of the windmill until the plane of the blades is perpendicular to the wind and the blades can extract maximum power from the wind. Given the rising price of oil, we may expect to see more and more windmills. Back five and six hundred years ago they were used extensively for grinding grain and pumping water—both tasks that could be done at the wind's convenience provided only the average rate was high enough. So the miller was concerned not so much with keeping a constant shaft speed but with keeping the blades facing into the wind. Some of the old mills were fascinating. The caps, carrying the arms and the blades, were so heavy that a simple vane was not powerful enough to swivel the apparatus around. One solution was to hitch up oxen to a long pole and use them to swivel the mill, but that required that the miller get up in the middle of the night (when else would wind change direction), get out of his nice warm bed, and hitch up the oxen, etc. Much better an automatic device, which

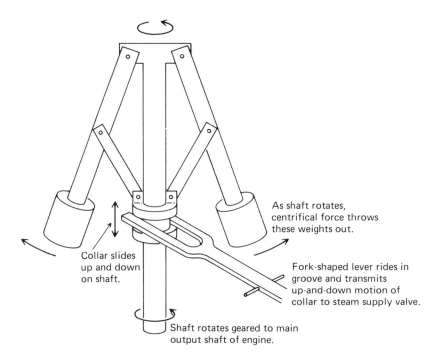

As shaft rotates,
centrifical force throws
these weights out.

Collar slides
up and down
on shaft.

Fork-shaped lever rides in
groove and transmits
up-and-down motion of
collar to steam supply valve.

Shaft rotates geared to main
output shaft of engine.

Figure 8.1 *Simplified diagram of a fly ball governor.*

they promptly invented.[*] Figure 8.2 shows a top view of a mill. On an arm sticking out the back side of the cap of the mill, there is an auxiliary fan that is geared down and connected to a pinion that engages a fixed ring gear on the top of the mill building just under the cap. When the wind blows at an angle to the auxiliary fan, the fan turns, the gears gear, the pinion pins, and the whole cap is cranked around its pivot. If the miller is clever enough and hooks up the gears the right way, it turns in the right direction to bring the main blades into the wind and the auxiliary fan once again perpendicular to the wind, at which point it stops turning, and the whole apparatus comes to rest (except the main blades, of course) without even waking the miller. If the wind is so light it won't turn the auxiliary fan, it won't do much for the main blades either, so forget it.

The people who specialize in the history of technology spend many happy hours arguing over the earliest recorded appearance of feedback control. For example, most of them would agree that Watt's governor is an example of feedback, and that a simple vane used to steer a windmill is not, but they part company over the above example. In order to be able to participate fully in the argument, you need some definitions (see Figure 8.3).

---

[*]   Note that grinding grain requires constant attention to prevent the grain from burning and the stones from wrecking each other, but water pumping could and did go on unattended.

WHY STUDY SERVOMECHANISMS?

With the dramatic decline in price of computers over the past ten years, they have moved out of the accounting departments of business and the ivy-covered walls of academia into private homes and industrial assembly lines. One of the major applications of the new micros has been, and will continue to be, in controlling physical devices of one sort or another. Now the fundamental idea behind a servomechanism is the application of feedback to controlling position or velocity or some other attribute of the device in question. In principle all one needs are three things. First, you need a sensor to measure the difference between where you are and where you want to be. This difference is called the "error" signal. Second, you need an actuator of some kind (perhaps a motor) that can affect the world. Third, you need a controller that will look at the error signal and, based on what it sees, drive the actuator in the direction that will decrease the error. Then with time, the error will get smaller, and you will approach ever more closely the desired state of the world. But sometimes errors can be dangerous or expensive if they are allowed to persist for any length of time, and it is desirable to reduce the error to zero as rapidly as possible. And here is where the world begins to get complicated, and we have to know something about the dynamics of the situation. In particular, the inertia of physical devices becomes a problem. Once you get a piece of machinery in motion, you can't say "stop" and have it come instantly to a halt just as the error signal reaches zero. It's going to keep on moving until the combined forces of friction and the actuator can slow it down to a stop, and by then you are way past the desired point and will have to turn around and retrace your path. If you want to control real devices properly, you have to worry about this type of problem .

The symbol Θ_o (pronounced "theta out") is the output variable that we wish to control. The symbol Θ_i (theta in) is the input variable whose value is given to us by God or somebody else more powerful than we are. It is sometimes called the "command variable."

Then a feedback control device or a "servomechanism" is one for which the following are true.

1. It tries to make Θ_o equal to Θ_i.

2. The energy associated with the output (or the change in the output) is not derived from the input signal.

3. The "effective cause" (but not necessarily the response of the device) must be proportional to the error signal ϵ, where

$$\epsilon \equiv \Theta_i - \Theta_o .$$

Clearly Watt's governor meets all these criteria. The command signal Θ_i is set by positioning the whole governor up or down relative to the takeoff lever. The fly balls compare the desired speed with the achieved speed and develop an error signal proportional to the difference. If Watt had hired a clockmaker or watch-

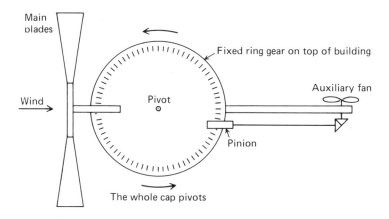

Figure 8.2 *An old windmill steering device, top view. The ring gear is fixed to the top of the mill building, and the cap, the main blades, and the auxiliary fan turn.*

maker to construct his governor, it would have absorbed a vanishingly small amount of power from either the input or the output signals and could have controlled an engine of arbitrarily large power. The source of energy to turn the shaft was clearly the steam supply and not the command signal.

How about the auxiliary fan steering device for the windmill. Θ_i is the wind direction, Θ_o the angle of the windmill cap, and the auxiliary fan rotates at a speed proportional to the difference between the two angles, but it seems to us that it takes the power necessary to move the cap from the input signal. Imagine that the auxiliary fan was replaced by a vane that could close electrical contacts to control an electric motor that would be geared to the ring gear to cause the cap to turn. Now it's clear. The energy to rotate the cap comes from the power lines, not from the wind signal.

We have spent so much time with these two simple devices so that you can get an initial feel for what feedback involves before we plunge into the bottomless pit ahead.

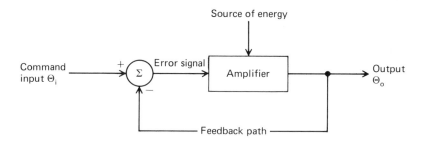

Figure 8.3 *Diagram of a feedback control system.*

Back in the eleventh century the Arabs had very complex water-pressure–operated automatons. One was a figure of a maiden who would come forward with a towel and a bowl of water and wash a guest's hands. Now the maiden's actions were entirely preprogrammed (built into her cams and levers and valves), and she would go through the same washing motions no matter what the size of the hands she was presented with. Indeed, she was perfectly happy to "wash" empty air if no hands at all were presented. She didn't have any feedback to tell her where the guest was or how dirty his hands were, either. Successful robots must sense their environments and modify their behavior according to the state of the world around them. In this chapter we are going to set our sights a little lower than designing a full-scale robot capable of independent action. What we are going to try to do is to understand the simplest form of feedback control system. We will consider a system about on a par with Watt's steam engine governor. There will be a 12-volt slot-car motor controlled by a power amplififer, controlled in turn by a DAC output from our computer. The output of the DAC will constitute the error signal applied to the amplifier to control the motor. On the motor shaft we will have a gear with a notch cut out of it so that a pair of photo darlingtons (electric eyes) can peak through to detect whether the notch is in front of them letting light in or not. Figure 8.4 is a block diagram of the mechanics, and Figures 8.5 and 8.6 show some details of the electronics.

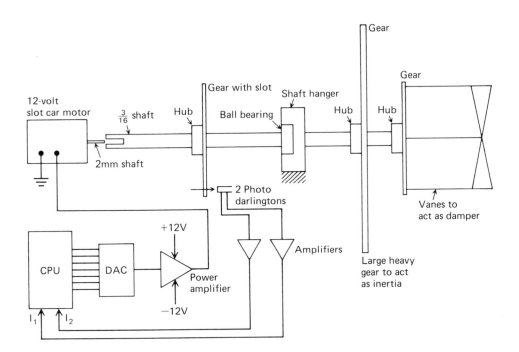

Figure 8.4 *Block diagram of servomechanism.*

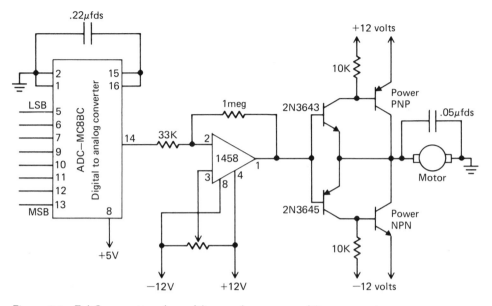

Figure 8.5 *DAC, operational amplifier, and power amplifier connections.*

We chose to count shaft revolutions with the photo cells rather than to measure shaft position for two reasons. First was expense. Ten-turn potentiometers of low friction are expensive. So are other devices for measuring position. Second was the fact that we are going to put these devices in the hands of less than expert programmers so that it might just be possible for the motor to be winding up to full speed just as the mechanical stop at the end of the tenth turn was reached. Something breaks or bends. In real life this problem must be faced and solved. For experimentation, such as we are doing here, we will simply sidestep the problem and use photocells. With photocells to count shaft revolutions, one can easily get accuracies of one part in 2^{16} (65,000) by double-precision counting, and there aren't any stops or ends-of-travel devices to worry about. We employed two photocells set side by side so that when cell A was triggered, we could look at cell B to see if it had "seen the light" yet. If it had, the shaft is rotating clockwise, and if not, the shaft is rotating counterclockwise. In one case we add to the shaft position counter; in the other we subtract.

Now clearly what we want to do is see where the shaft is (as indicated by the software-maintained-shaft-counter). Compare that to the command shaft position (Θ_i), which is a number we are storing inside the computer or reading in from some analog or digital input device. Depending on the result of the comparison, we tell the motor to turn in a direction that will decrease the error, and when the shaft gets to the right place, we stop. Only there is a problem. Just because we told the motor it needn't run any more doesn't mean it came to an instant stop. There is such a thing as inertia that will keep it turning. There are also damping forces that will bring the system to a stop. In fact, we have quite a complicated mechanical system here, which we are going to have to analyze before we can predict its behavior accurately. Before we tackle this real system, let us look first at a much simpler abstract system that can be analyzed mathematically. Then we will see how well or how poorly our system compares.

DEFINING SOME TERMS

We need to introduce a few terms from the field of physics before we can study even a simple servomechanism. As you may or may not remember from a high school physics course, the fundamental equation of mechanics is

$$F = ma,$$

where F is a force, m is the mass of an object, and a is the acceleration the object will undergo. Force, of course, is a measure of how hard you push against the object. Mass is a measure of how much material there is in the object, and the acceleration is the rate of change of the velocity. If you accelerate at 5 feet per second per second, then after one second you are moving at 5 feet per second, after two seconds you are moving at 10 feet per second, and after 10 seconds you will be moving with a velocity of 50 feet per second.

Velocity, in turn, is the rate of change of position. If you are moving at a constant velocity (no acceleration) of 10 feet per second, then in 17 seconds you will cover a distance of 170 feet. Putting all this into more formal terms, we write that

$$v = \frac{d}{dt}(x) = \dot{x}$$

and

$$a = \frac{d}{dt}(v) = \dot{v} = \frac{d^2}{dt^2}(x) = \ddot{x}.$$

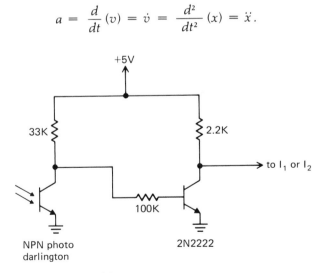

Figure 8.6 *Photo darlington amplifiers.*

DERIVATIVES

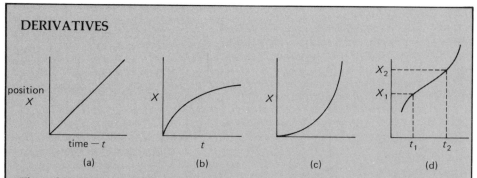

position
X

time — t

(a)   (b)   (c)   (d)

These three curves are plots of the position of three automobiles as a function of time. Automobile (a) is driving at a constant speed, (b) is slowing down to a stop, and (c) is speeding up. How can we tell that? Look at (d). At time t_1 the car is at position x_1, and at time t_2 the car has moved to position x_2. Suppose the difference between t_1 and t_2 is one second and the difference between x_1 and x_2 is 88 feet. Then we can say that the car moved 88 feet in one second, or 88 feet per second (or 60 miles per hour). This is the velocity of the car. Notice that in (a) we will get the same answer any place we measure the velocity. In (b) the car starts out covering a lot of ground every second, but after a while it doesn't move so far in a second. In (c) the reverse is true. The "steeper" the line is, the faster the car is moving. We measure velocity as the change in position divided by the change in time, or: $\Delta x / \Delta t$. If we take the two points (1 and 2) very close together, we can measure the velocity pretty accurately, even though the car may be changing speed. We can shorten up our notation as follows:

$$\frac{x_2 - x_1}{t_2 - t_1} = \frac{\Delta x}{\Delta t} \simeq \dot{x},$$

where $\dot{x}$ (read "x dot") is the "derivative of position with respect to time," or more briefly, "the velocity."

If we plotted the velocity of a car versus time, we could similarly measure "the derivative of velocity with respect to time," or the "acceleration": a. For example:

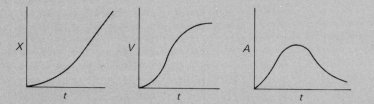

X   V   A

t   t   t

The position of the car (x) changes slowly at first and then more rapidly. If we look at the slope of the line of x versus t, we see that in the beginning the velocity is small, but it increases and then levels off at a constant velocity. (The x versus t curve has a constant slope—it is a straight line.) Looking at the derivative of the velocity curve (the acceleration), we find it first increasing and then falling back to zero when the velocity becomes constant.

That is, velocity is the derivative with respect to time of position (x) (the "time rate of change" of position) and is symbolized for brevity as $\dot{x}$ (read "x dot"). Acceleration is the time rate of change of velocity (symbolized as $\dot{v}$) or, since v itself is the derivative of distance with respect to time, we can write acceleration as the second derivative of position with respect to time and use $\ddot{x}$ (x double dot) as a shorthand notation.

Suppose this mass we are trying to accelerate has a large sail attached to it that is perpendicular to the direction we want to move in and, hence, as we begin to go faster acts as a drag opposing our acceleration. In fact, if we stopped pushing, the air resistance, or what is called "viscous damping," will gradually bring the mass to rest. Now we have two forces acting on the mass. There is P, the push you are giving it, and D, the drag of air resistance. It is the difference between these forces that determines the acceleration. It is the difference because one (P) is acting to increase the velocity, and the other (D) is acting to decrease the velocity. So the net force acting will be

$$F = P - D,$$

and it is the net force that will determine the acceleration. So we can write

$$F = P - D = ma$$

or

$$P = ma + D.$$

Now we are going to make an assumption that is not quite true in the real world but is very convenient mathematically. We are going to assume that the drag (D) is linearly proportional to the velocity. In real life, drag is roughly proportional to the square of the velocity, but for small values of velocity we can approximate this with a linear relationship. So

$$D = fv = f\dot{x},$$

where f is the "damping coefficient," determined in our case by the size of the sail. The larger the "sail," the larger f will be.

Rewriting everything we get

$$P = ma + D,$$

or

$$P = m\ddot{x} + f\dot{x}.$$

This is a "differential equation" relating the external force (P) applied to the object to the acceleration ($\ddot{x}$) and velocity ($\dot{x}$) of the object and to its mass (m) and the damping coefficient (f).

Let us try to get a feel for the underlying physics of the situation. Suppose you push against a heavy railway car with constant force. In the beginning the car is standing still, but gradually you overcome inertia and the car goes faster and faster. If you could run fast enough to keep up with it and keep on applying your constant push, you would find that after a while you are having less and less success accelerating the car. Wind resistance is beginning to fight against you. Finally, if you kept on pushing long enough, the car would reach a velocity where the wind resistance was just equal and opposite to your push, and thereafter the car would move with constant velocity. If you wanted to go faster, you would have to push harder. If you pushed less strongly, the car would slow down, because the drag exceeded the push.

In the next section we are going to complicate life in two ways. First, we are going to make the external force P vary depending on what the system is doing. We will use a computer to control the force P. Second, we are going to go from linear coordinates to circular coordinates. Forces will be replaced by torques trying to turn shafts, and mass will be replaced by the "moment of inertia"—the resistance of the shaft and its associated parts to angular acceleration.

In circular coordinates, position (x) is replaced by shaft angle (Θ), velocity (V) by ω (omega), and acceleration by angular acceleration α (alpha).

As before,

$$\alpha = \dot{\omega} = \ddot{\Theta}$$

and

$$\omega = \dot{\Theta}.$$

ANALYSIS OF A SIMPLE SERVOMECHANISM

Consider a system similar to that shown in Figure 8.3, which has a motor that generates a torque, a viscous damper, but no inertia to speak of. That torque is proportional to the error signal applied to the input of the amplifier. Thus τ (read "tau") is given by

$$\tau_m = \epsilon \cdot \mu,$$

where μ is a constant dependent on the particular amplifier and motor we have, and ϵ is the error signal.

The other torque we are going to consider at this point is that caused by viscous damping. That is a "drag" such as that generated by a fan. This drag is assumed to be proportional to the speed of rotation:

$$\tau_d = f\dot{\Theta}_o,$$

where the dot indicates differentiation with respect to time, so $\dot{\Theta}$ is the angular velocity (ω) measured in radians per second. Remember that there are 2π radians per $360°$, so $\dot{\Theta}/2\pi$ is the number of revolutions per second the output shaft is making.

At any instant in time the sum of the torques about the output shaft must equal zero. Since the motor and the damping are working in opposite directions, one tending to speed up the shaft and the other tending to slow it down, we may write

$$f \dot{\Theta}_o - \mu (\Theta_i - \Theta_o) = 0. \qquad (8.1)$$

In case you are interested, this is a linear, first-order differential equation. We can divide by μ and rearrange the equation to get

$$\frac{f}{\mu} \dot{\Theta}_o + \Theta_o = \Theta_i. \qquad (8.2)$$

It turns out this servo acts just like a low-pass filter with a time constant of $f/\mu = T$. If Θ_i is a step function changing from zero to one when $t = 0$, then the output has the form

$$\Theta_o = A + Be^{-t/T},$$

and Figure 8.7 shows the behavior.

What we are saying here is that if we suddenly request the system to move from angle 1 to angle 2, it will approach angle 2 rapidly at first and then ever more slowly creep into position. Why? Because in the beginning there is a large difference between the actual position (Θ_o) and the command position (Θ_i). This means a big error term applied to the input of the amplifier, which means the amplifier will put out a large voltage, which will try hard to turn the motor and the shaft. The only other force we are considering is the viscous damping, so the shaft will increase its speed until the point where the drag forces equal the torque generated by the motor.

As the actual shaft position approaches the desired shaft position, the error will become smaller. This will decrease the voltage from the amplifier and, hence, the torque the motor generates. The shaft will slow down until the drag equals the

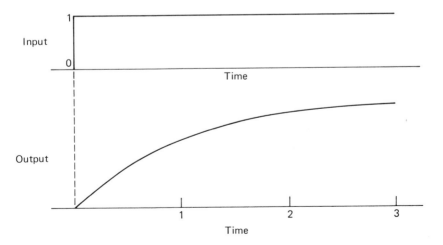

Figure 8.7 *Response to a step function of a servo with viscous damping and no inertia.*

motor torque. But by now we are even closer to the desired angle, and the shaft will turn even slower and then yet more slowly, finally creeping toward the desired position and actually reaching it only after an infinite time. The error is reduced to $1/e$ of its initial value after T seconds. The ultimate error is zero, for given enough time, we can see from Equation 8.2 that Θ_o—the angular velocity—is equal to zero if and only if the output is equal to the input.

Now let us consider a *ramp* input. That is, suppose Θ_i is a linear function of time:

$$\Theta_i = at \qquad \text{or} \qquad \dot{\Theta}_i = a \; .$$

Look back at Equation 8.1. In order to turn the output shaft at a fixed velocity, we must overcome the drag due to the viscous damping. This requires a torque proportional to the angular velocity and the damping coefficient f. But the only place a torque can form is from a nonzero term amplified by the amplifier. So in order to keep turning, the error must be nonzero. Assuming that the output will follow the input except for a lag of Φ, we get

$$\Theta_o = \Theta_i - \Phi$$

or

$$\Theta_i - \Theta_o = \Phi$$

and

$$\dot{\Theta}_o = \dot{\Theta}_i = a \; .$$

Substituting these in Equation 8.1, we have

$$\Phi = \frac{af}{\mu} \; .$$

Figure 8.8 shows this performance.

Suppose that instead of a ramp input we wrap a rope around a pulley fixed to the output shaft and then hang a weight from the rope, providing a fixed torque load τ_ϱ. Let us wait until everything comes to rest and see what has happened. The angular velocity will be zero, so the damping term drops out, and balancing torques, we have

$$\mu(\Theta_i - \Theta_o) = \tau_\varrho \; ,$$

or

$$\epsilon = \frac{\tau_\varrho}{\mu} \; .$$

By raising the gain of the amplifier (μ), we can reduce the magnitude of the error due to a fixed torque load, but we can't bring it to zero. The same is true of the error (lag) in the response to a ramp input.

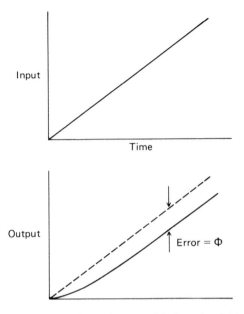

Figure 8.8 *Lag response to a ramp input (servo with damping but no inertia).*

To summarize these points, for a first order servo with viscous damping:

1. The error is zero for constant input.
2. The error is nonzero for ramp input.
3. The error is nonzero for constant torque load.

A SECOND-ORDER SERVO

To the motor and the damping of the system we have just considered, let us add inertia (see Figure 8.9). Inertia resists acceleration. Angular acceleration is the second derivative of the angle with respect to time, and the "resistance to acceleration" appears as a torque proportional to the "moment of inertia" times the angular acceleration. (The moment of inertia of a disk or cylinder is proportional to the square of the radius times the mass and is symbolized by I.) Adding this term to Equation 8.1, we get

$$I\,\ddot{\Theta}_o + f\dot{\Theta}_o - \mu(\Theta_i - \Theta_o) = 0 \,.$$

This equation has three terms in it, each representing a torque about the output shaft. The first term $(I\,\ddot{\Theta}_o)$ reflects the effects of inertia, which tries to keep the speed of rotation constant. When you try to change the speed of rotation—try to produce an angular acceleration—the inertia resists this change. The second term $(f\,\dot{\Theta}_o)$ is the damping term. This is the effect of the frictional forces, which try to bring the system to rest with zero angular velocity. Finally, the term $\mu(\Theta_i - \Theta_o)$ represents the torque generated by the motor, which is proportional to the error.

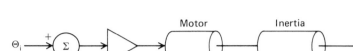

Figure 8.9 *A second-order servomechanism with both inertia and damping.*

The inertia and the viscous damping both resist increases in speed, and the motor torque aids such an increase. This accounts for the signs of the various terms. We can define a couple of new terms for mathematical convenience:

$$\omega_n = \sqrt{\frac{\mu}{I}} = \text{the "natural" frequency,}$$

and

$$\delta = \frac{f}{2\,\mu I} \equiv \text{the damping ratio.}$$

Then substituting these in, we get

$$\frac{1}{\omega_n^2}\,\ddot{\Theta}_o + \frac{2\delta}{\omega_n}\,\dot{\Theta}_o + \Theta_o = \Theta_i.$$

If we look at a step-function input, we get basically two different types of behavior, depending on the value of δ, the damping ratio. If δ is less than *one,* the system is said to be underdamped, and we get oscillations as shown in Figure 8.10. The smaller δ is, the bigger the oscillations. The period of the oscillations is

$$\frac{2\pi}{\omega_n} \qquad \text{or} \qquad 2\pi\,\sqrt{\frac{I}{\mu}}\,.$$

The period gets longer if the inertia increases and gets shorter if the amplifier gain increases.

When δ = 1, there is no overshoot, and the system is said to be "critically damped." For larger δ the response becomes more and more sluggish, and the system is said to be "overdamped."

The response of a second-order servo to steady-state and ramp inputs and to torque loads is the same as that of a first-order system, because with constant or linear input, the acceleration term goes to zero, and the effects of the inertia disappear.

Exercise 8.1

Let us see how our real servo system differs from the ideal one we have considered up to now. The major difference is in the response of the motor to signals from the DAC. The main problem is something called "stiction," which means "sticky friction." It takes a reasonably large current to get the motor to move at all. Then once it starts turning, a relatively modest increase in current will cause a dramatic increase in speed. Then after a while an increase in current has very little effect, and the motor doesn't go much faster because it is "saturated." But what we want to discover is not really the speed of the motor but rather its torque as a function of the applied voltage.

Let us assume that for small angular velocities the only forces affecting our system will be the motor torque and the resistance to acceleration caused by inertia. Then if this is indeed the case, we find that

$$\Theta = \frac{1}{2}\,\alpha t^2,$$

where $\alpha = \tau/I$, that is, motor torque divided by inertia equals the angular acceleration. First of all, we output a value of 128 from our computer into the DAC of Figure 8.6 and adjust the amplifier bias so that the voltage across the motor is zero. At time $t = 0$, change the output voltage to some other value V by putting another

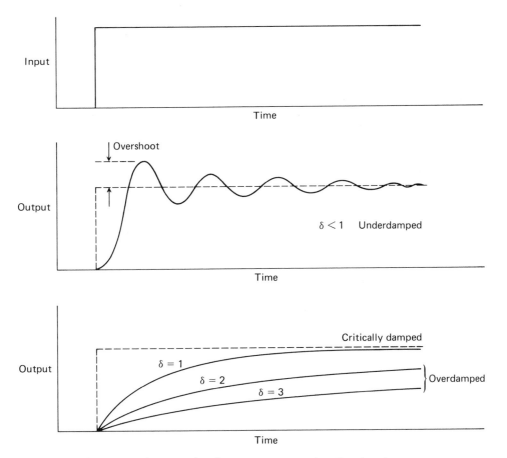

Figure 8.10 *Response of a second-order servo to a step-function input.*

number in the output register. Suggested trial numbers are 128 ± 16, ± 32, ± 64, + 127 and − 128. At time $t = 0$, start a timer and measure the time of the first exposure of photocell A (t_1), the time that same photocell is exposed again one revolution later (t_2), and the time it is exposed for the third time (t_3) after a second full revolution. Your time should be measured in milliseconds with a range of up to 5 seconds. One way to do this is to set up a one-millisecond repeating timer, and when it "ticks," increment a 16-bit counter. This might be done as an interrupt routine. Since you have nothing else to do, you might just as well poll the photocell, waiting for it to see light. Figure 8.11 shows some pseudocode that would do the job on our pseudomachine. After the third time is measured, you should turn off the motor so it can coast to a stop and print out or otherwise display the three values of time you have measured. After the motor comes to rest, you should try a different value of V.

Having measured t_1, t_2, and t_3 for several values of V, you can now calculate the acceleration of the motor as a function of V and hence the torque as a function of the applied voltage V. How? We assume that for low speeds the only torques acting on the shaft are the motor torque and the resistance to changes in angular velocity due to the inertia of the system. Thus,

$$\tau_m = I \ddot{\Theta}_o .$$

We don't know the moment of inertia of the system (I), but we know it is fixed, so we can measure τ_m/I and be happy with that. Calling

$$\frac{\tau_m}{I} = \alpha ,$$

we have

$$\ddot{\Theta} = \alpha ,$$

$$\dot{\Theta} = \alpha t ,$$

$$\Theta = \frac{1}{2} \alpha t^2 ,$$

which are, of course, the standard equations of motion of an object subjected to a constant force (as, for instance, a free-falling body accelerated by gravity). We don't know the angle the shaft was sitting at when we first turned on the motor, because all we can tell is when the notch passes the photocell. But we do know the time it took to get there. We know that

$$\Theta_1 = \frac{1}{2} \alpha t_1^2 ,$$

and we have two unknowns: α and Θ_1. But we also know at what time the shaft got to Θ_2, one full revolution past Θ_1. That was t_2. So we can write

$$\Theta_2 = \frac{1}{2} \alpha t_2^2 .$$

```
LOOK:   INPUT      PHOTOCELL      Wait for photocell to
        BZA        LOOK           see the light.
        LDA        TIMER          Save the value in the timer
        STAX       TIME           in T₀, T₁, and T₂.
HOLD:   INPUT      PHOTOCELL      Wait for photocell to
        BNA        HOLD           go dark.
        INX                       Increment X.
        TXA
        SUBIM      3              Do this 3 times.
        BMA        LOOK
        LDAIM      128            Turn off the
        OUTPUT     MOTOR          motor.
        HLT                       Stop.
```

Figure 8.11 *Code to record times at which the photocell sees the light for the first three revolutions.*

Taking the difference between these two equations, we have

$$\Theta_2 - \Theta_1 = \frac{1}{2} \, \alpha(t_2^2 - t_1^2),$$

and remembering that $\Theta_2 - \Theta_1$ is one full shaft revolution or 2π radians, we can write that

$$\alpha = \frac{4\pi}{t_2^2 - t_1^2}.$$

But the same relationships hold between Θ_2 and Θ_3 and t_2 and t_3, so we can compute another value for α:

$$\alpha' = \frac{4\pi}{t_3^2 - t_2^2}.$$

If our assumptions of no friction and linearity, etc., were correct, α should equal α' for all values of V. Do they? Plot a curve of the average of α and α' versus V. Is the motor symmetric in its torque in both directions? Is torque a linear function of V? How could you arrange to generate a torque that was a linear function of an error signal? What is the smallest value of V that will cause the shaft to rotate at all?

Exercise 8.2 Experiment on Closed Loop

We are now ready to "close the loop" and have the computer control the motor so that we have a feedback system. For convenience let us define $128 + V$ as the number we put into the DAC to control the motor torque. Positive V (numbers in the DAC greater than 128) will cause the motor to turn in a "positive" direction.

That may correspond to photocell 2 being already on when photocell 1 first sees the light, or it may correspond to photocell 2 still being in the dark. That will depend on how your servo is wired up. Negative V (numbers in the DAC less than 128) will cause the motor to turn in the other—the "negative"—direction. If you like, you may say that positive is clockwise and negative is counterclockwise. You just have to choose the proper end of the shaft to look at.

The second variable we need to define is N, which is the number of shaft revolutions we are *away* from some arbitrary point. When you first turn the system on, you set $V = 0$ to allow the motor to come to a stop, and then after a couple of seconds in which you didn't count a shaft revolution, you declare the shaft to be in the "home" position or at a count of 128. Perhaps it might be easier to let the motor turn the shaft until whatever count you have goes to 128 and then declare the system ready to run. Set the command position to be $128 + N$ for 5 seconds, then $128 - N$ for 5 seconds, and back and forth, generating a square wave for the output shaft to follow. Try Ns of 5, 10, and 20.

To close the loop, we take the difference between the command position and the actual shaft position (as counted by photocell interrupts) and call that the error signal. Using this error signal, we look up in a table to discover what V to put out to generate a torque linearly proportional to the error. We output that value V, and if we have our directions right, the motor spins the shaft, the error decreases, and the output shaft assumes the position the command told it to take.

You will have to consider carefully how to arrange the table that gives you torque as a function of error. For small errors (± 1 or 2) we need to apply enough torque so that the shaft will turn, however slowly, to bring the error to zero. Having measured the minimum V that will cause motion, you know what values to put in here. At the other end you might decide that you are going to try to be linear over the range of errors from zero to ± 64 and just put out full force at any error of 64 or greater.

For command positions of 128 ± 10, observe the overshoot as the shaft turns too far, reverses, comes back and undershoots and narrows down its error in the fashion of Figure 8.11. Include in your program a section of code that will measure the largest excursion of the shaft beyond the command position, and print this value out.

Add a large gear or other mass with high inertia to the shaft to increase the inertia of the system. (Watch out for the teeth on this gear. They are going to be turning quite fast at times and will give a pretty good imitation of a buzz saw if they get half a chance.) Now measure the overshoot both by program and by eye. You will see that the frequency of oscillation is lower and the overshoot is greater. Once you get that big gear turning, it is going to take some time to bring it to a stop.

Take off the big gear and replace it with a model airplane propeller or a set of damping vanes. This should cut down on the overshoot by increasing the damping constant δ. Is there much actual change in behavior? Try the system with both the big gear and the damping vanes. What now? Set N to zero so that the command position is a constant 128 with no change. Put on the big gear and arrange a string over some teeth and then wrap it a couple of dozen times around the shaft in a smooth tight helix. Attach a 4-oz fishing sinker or other weight to the end of the string, and slowly let the string take up the weight. The output shaft will turn, lowering the weight, until the error is large enough to generate a torque big enough to oppose the torque applied by the weight. How many turns does the shaft make, and what is the output voltage level? Given the radius of the shaft and the size of the weight, you can calculate the torque the weight applies ($\tau_\omega = W \cdot R$ in inch ounces). If the weight is 4 oz and the radius of the shaft is 3/32, then the torque is $4 \times 3/32 = 3/8$ inch ounces. Drum your fingers on the servo system board so that the vibration will perhaps release any "stickiness" before you take your measurements. You can use the value you measured here to calibrate your curve of torque versus voltage. Mind you, this is a static as opposed to a dynamic measurement, but at least it's better than nothing.

Measuring the lag in response to a ramp input is not worth the effort, so we will skip that.

9 Fancier Controls

In the previous chapter our computer existed purely for the purpose of taking the difference between the input and the output and translating that to a linear value of applied torque. In this chapter we will try to use it in somewhat fancier ways to see if we can't improve the overall performance of the system.

The three classical methods of improving servomechanism performance are called derivative feedback, error-rate control, and integral control. They are classical (that is, pre-microcomputer) because they can be made from ordinary resistors and capacitors and because their behavior is mathematically tractable. That is, we can predict in equation form what will happen when. Now it is nice and neat and cosy to be able to write down an equation that will predict the behavior of a system under all conditions, fair weather or foul, at dark or full of the moon, but it isn't a good idea to make a religion out of it. Consider, as Rudyard Kipling would have you do, the "way of a man with a maid" or—not to be too sexist about it—the way of a maid with a man. I will go to my grave believing that no equation will ever be written that will describe the behavior of either party. But that does not automatically make the situation an uninteresting one.

Remember, as well, that microcomputers *do* exist now, and that they can do some pretty fancy manipulations of numbers to generate some pretty fancy behavior. We will examine that more closely in the next chapter.

DERIVATIVE FEEDBACK

The first "fancy" system we will look at is called derivative control. Figure 9.1 shows a block diagram of a system. There is an amplifier, some inertia, and some viscous damping with regular feedback of the output signal to generate a term equal to

$$\Theta_i - \Theta_o .$$

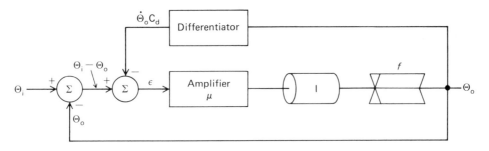

Figure 9.1 *A servo with derivative feedback.*

In addition, we have a box at the top of the diagram that measures the output shaft position and generates a signal proportional to the angular velocity of the shaft $\dot{\Theta}$. A tachometer is such a device, or a small electric motor/generator will put out a voltage proportional to the RPM of the shaft. Since this signal is so easy to generate, derivative control is or was popular to apply. Besides, it does actually improve performance somewhat.

Adding in the derivative term, as shown in Figure 9.1, gives the error the form

$$\epsilon = \Theta_i - \Theta_o - C_d \dot{\Theta}_o,$$

and plugging that into the differential equation of motion, we get

$$I \ddot{\Theta}_o + f \dot{\Theta}_o - \mu(\Theta_i - \Theta_o - C_d \dot{\Theta}_o) = 0.$$

Rearranging terms, we get

$$I \ddot{\Theta}_o + (f + \mu C_d)\dot{\Theta}_o + \mu\Theta_o = \mu\Theta_i.$$

This is the same equation of motion we had before for a second-order system with the damping term replaced by $f + \mu C_d$ instead of just f. Solving for the damping ratio δ, we have

$$\delta = \frac{f + \mu C_d}{2\sqrt{\mu I}}.$$

Derivative feedback has the effect of increasing the damping of a system, thus reducing overshoot and oscillation. If a real system is well made, viscous damping is typically very low compared with motor torque and inertia. One uses ball bearings and streamlined design to make sure that this is so. One hates to then add intentional viscous damping just to reduce oscillation. If the system is being run from batteries and the energy supply is limited, adding viscous damping will cause that energy to be dissipated in fighting friction. If one adds derivative control instead, no actual energy is dissipated beating the air around, and the batteries will last a lot longer.

How would we go about adding derivative control to our servo system? Using a one-shot counter or a clock, one can readily measure the amount of time necessary to complete a full revolution. Using table look up or using a "reciprocation" routine, one can translate this period of time into an angular velocity. Table look up is perhaps easier. You round off the time to complete one revolution to five bits of accuracy (a number between 0 and 31) and use that as an index to look up the RPM in a table built for the occasion.

Exercise 9.1

Add derivative feedback to the system of the previous chapter. Adjust the entries in the table (the amount of derivative feedback) till the system is just *not* oscillating (critically damped). How much derivative feedback was required? Has the response to a constant torque load changed?

ERROR-RATE CONTROL

Another way of changing the apparent amount of damping in a system is by adding to the equation of motion a term that is proportional to the derivative of the error. Figure 9.2 shows the system, and the equation of motion is

$$I\,\ddot{\Theta}_o + f\,\dot{\Theta}_o - \mu(\Theta_i - \Theta_o + C_e\dot{\Theta}_i - C_e\dot{\Theta}_o) = 0.$$

Rearranging, we get

$$I\,\ddot{\Theta}_o + (f + \mu C_e)\,\dot{\Theta}_o + \mu\Theta_o = \mu\Theta_i + \mu C_e\dot{\Theta}_i.$$

Because of the $f + \mu C_e$ term on the left-hand side, we find that error-rate control decreases oscillation, just as derivative feedback and genuine viscous damping do. But the $\dot{\Theta}_i$ term on the right-hand side means that if f is small with respect to μC_e, then there is no error when following a ramp input. Steady-state error due to torque loading is unchanged.

Exercise 9.2

Implementing error-rate control in a computer such as ours is easier than implementing derivative control. We keep an old value of the difference between Θ_i and Θ_o. Call it OLD ERROR. We compute a new value for that difference called NEW ERROR. Then the rate of change of the error term is given by

NEW ERROR − OLD ERROR.

We add this to the value of NEW ERROR, getting an index to use to look up what voltage to output. Thus the index will be

IND = 2 * NEW ERROR − OLD ERROR.

Every few milliseconds we compute a new index and a new output voltage and put the current NEW ERROR into the variable called OLD ERROR and compute a new value for NEW ERROR. Actually, with the fairly coarse scheme we have of

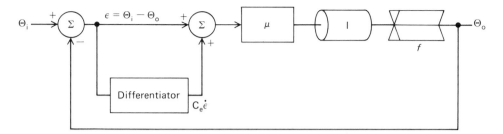

Figure 9.2 *Error-rate control.*

measuring the output shaft position, the derivative of the error is going to jump around a lot as we click in one more revolution or not. But that is the major drawback of error-rate control, anyway. Even if we were to measure shaft position with a potentiometer, the variation in value of the voltage from angle to angle would not be smooth, and taking the derivative of such a noisy function only accentuates the problem.

INTEGRAL CONTROL

The third classical method of modifying servo behavior is to add to the error a term that is proportional to the integral over time of the difference between Θ_i and Θ_o. This is sometimes called integral control or "reset" control. Figure 9.3 shows the diagram, and the equation is

$$I\,\ddot{\Theta}_o + f\,\dot{\Theta}_o - \mu\epsilon - \mu C_i \int_{-\infty}^{t} \epsilon \; dt = 0,$$

where $\epsilon = \Theta_i - \Theta_o$.

Without going into the mathematical details, we can state that the addition of the integral term means that the longer an error persists, the larger that term will become and the stronger will be the torque attempting to eliminate that error. Therefore, for both ramp imputs and constant torque loads, the integral term will gradually grow until the error is reduced to zero and eliminated. But a little thought will show that the addition of integral control will tend to make the servo system unstable and oscillatory. Consider. We have been to the left of the command point for some time, so the integral of the error has built up until it is quite large. We approach the command point, and the error term reduces toward zero, calling for less and less power output, so we will slow down as we approach the command point and stop with little or no overshoot. But no! The integral term is still large and demanding strong forces moving us to the right. We overshoot and the forces are still rightward. We have to have an error of the opposite sign (too far to the right) large enough and long enough to almost cancel out the former value of the integral before the force will be back toward the command point again. Clearly, this can lead to run-away oscillation if we aren't careful.

But integral control not only eliminates ramp and torque load errors; it is seductively easy to implement in our computer. Every N microseconds we simply compute

$$INTEGRAL = INTEGRAL + ERROR.$$

And there it is, ready to go.

Exercise 9.3

Apply integral control to the system you have been dealing with.

Exercise 9.4

One way to improve stability and get the benefits of integral control is to combine that with error-rate control. This gives an equation for the error that looks like

$$E = \epsilon + C_e \dot{\epsilon} + C_i \int \epsilon \, dt,$$

where $\epsilon = \Theta_i - \Theta_o$ and E is the error term fed to the amplifier.

We will not go into the general problem of how to select C_e and C_i to ensure good response and also stability. That topic is beyond the scope of this book. One obvious special case is to keep C_i small with respect to one. A value near $1/16$ is easy to calculate and probably small enough to ensure stability. Pick a C_e around $1/4$ and see what kind of behavior your servo system exhibits when subjected to square wave input commands. Try $C_e = 1/2$ and $1/8$. Try $C_i = 1/8$ and $1/32$. Describe what you would expect first. Then try the experiments and compare what you saw with what you predicted. Set $C_e = 0$. How big can you make C_i before the system "runs away"?

BANG-BANG CONTROL

Up to now we have been looking at complicated and sophisticated schemes for improving feedback control systems. Let us now abandon all subtlety and do things in the simplest imaginable form. Let us program the computer as follows:

"If the error between the command and the actual shaft position is positive, we will turn the motor on *full force* in the direction that will reduce the error. If the error is negative, we will turn the motor on full force in the other direction. If the error is less than ±1/2 (equal to zero within the quantization noise of our system), we will turn the motor off."

The name of this approach is supposed to be an onomatopoetic reference to the noise it makes as it slams from full clockwise to full counterclockwise acceleration.

Does it work? Surprisingly enough it does, and reasonably well also. If there were no viscous damping and just the bang-bang motor and inertia, we would get a nondecaying oscillation, as shown in Figure 9.4. Note that the sections between crossings of the axis (between points of zero error) are sections of parabolas ($y = k x^2$) and not sine waves. With the addition of damping, the waves decay quite rapidly.

Exercise 9.5

Resurrect your linear servo program from Chapter 8, and change the output table to generate full motor power for any nonzero error; that is, if the error is positive, output a motor command signal of 0 or 255—whichever is the right direction; and for negative error, output the other. Measure the overshoot of the bare system, of the system with the added inertia, and of the system with the added damping. Use the same-sized square wave command you used in Chapter 8. Now compare the overshoot of bang-bang with the overshoot of the linear system. How much worse off (percentagewise) are you? How much did this simplicity of control (full on or full off) cost in performance?

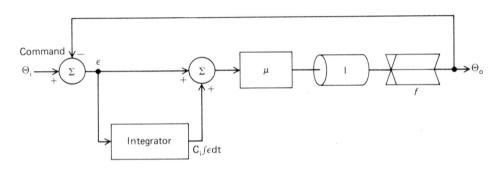

Figure 9.3 *Integral control.*

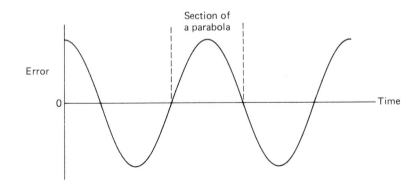

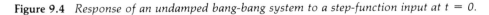

Figure 9.4 *Response of an undamped bang-bang system to a step-function input at $t = 0$.*

10 Optimum and Adaptive Control

At the end of the last chapter we introduced a very simple control strategy called bang-bang control. The reason is not *just* that we like simple things, although that certainly is true. The reason is that with this amazingly simple strategy we can dramatically improve the performance of our servo system when compared with a linear system. But it takes a computer to do the job right.

Before we can understand even bang-bang systems very well, let alone the more advanced systems we were mentioning, we have to take a side excursion to learn about phase space and nonlinear systems.

THE PHASE PLANE

Consider a second-order linear differential equation such as

$$\ddot{x} + k_1\dot{x} + k_2x = 0, \tag{10.1}$$

which says that the acceleration ($\ddot{x}$) plus a constant times the velocity ($\dot{x}$) plus another constant times the position (x) equals zero. Such an equation describes the motion of a mass-spring-damper system (see Figure 10.1) or a proportional servo with inertia, such as we discussed back in Chapter 8.

Let us look at the behavior of this system. Suppose we raise the mass upward a few inches from its rest position, and then release it. The spring has been allowed to shorten up, so the force it is exerting is diminished, but gravity is still pulling the mass downward. The mass begins to drop, accelerating under the net force of gravity minus the pull of the spring. As it accelerates, it moves downward, stretching the spring and increasing the pull of the spring. As the mass moves through the rest position, the two forces are equal (the spring upward and gravity downward), so the mass ceases to accelerate, and if it were not moving, it would stay in this position.

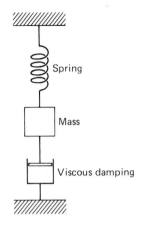

Figure 10.1 *A mass-spring-damper system.*

Now the force exerted by the spring is greater than the force of gravity, and the mass begins to decelerate and slow down. As the mass moves further down, the force exerted by the spring keeps on increasing, because the spring is being stretched ever longer. Because the net upward force is increasing, the mass decelerates more and more rapidly, eventually coming to rest some distance below the equilibrium point.

But it can't remain at rest with a net force acting on it. The spring begins to draw the mass upward. Again it accelerates until it passes the equilibrium point, where the force of gravity equals the pull of the spring, and it keeps on rising because of its inertia until it reaches a point slightly below the point at which you let it go. Then it begins dropping again, repeating the whole performance with somewhat smaller amplitudes. Each time it repeats the oscillation it is losing energy to the forces of air resistance and the viscous damper, which is really the equivalent of an automobile shock absorber. As it loses energy, its excursions become smaller and smaller until finally it comes to rest at the equilibrium point—the force of gravity just equal to the pull of the spring and the velocity equal to zero. Figure 10.2 is a picture of this behavior.

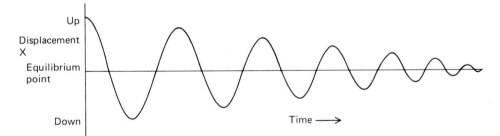

Figure 10.2 *The decaying oscillations of a mass-spring-damper system shown in the time domain.*

This is not the only way to represent the behavior of this system. We might plot the velocity of the mass as a function of time. Note that the velocity will become zero just at the points of greatest excursion, and it will be maximum when passing through the equilibrium point.

Yet a third way to display the behavior in pictorial form might be to plot the velocity versus the displacement. This is called a "phase plane analysis" and turns out to be very useful in the study of the simpler types of nonlinear systems, such as a bang-bang servo.

An equation such as (10.1) can be solved analytically if k_1 and k_2 are constants, but if they are functions of x or of time, then an analytic solution is highly unlikely. To make it possible to get some estimates of the behavior of such "nonlinear" systems, we introduce the "phase plane." We use the regular x-y plane of high school mathematics, but in this case we let y stand for the velocity and x stand for the position. Thus

$$y = \dot{x} = \frac{dx}{dt}.$$

If the system is moving toward the right (toward increasing x), then y must be positive (the velocity must be greater than zero). If the system is moving toward the left (toward decreasing x), y must be negative. If the system is moving fast, y will be large, and if it is moving slowly, y will be small. When y is zero, the system is standing still, although, of course, it may not stay that way very long, because there may be unbalanced external forces acting upon it. But there will in general be some x position at which the forces are all balanced and at which the system will reside happily, provided it gets there with zero velocity. We will move the origin of our x-axis along as required so that one of these "singular" points is at the origin.

Let us reexamine the mass spring damper in the phase plane.

Look at Figure 10.3. At point 1 we have a small positive x position, but the velocity is positive ($y > 0$), so we find x getting larger. The velocity is decreasing and the system is slowing down (y is getting smaller), so pretty soon we reach the furthest excursion in x, when for an instant the system stops moving ($y = 0$). Then y becomes negative and the system starts moving toward the left—toward smaller values of x. Notice that whenever $y > 0$, the system must move to the right—never left—and when $y < 0$ (below the x-axis), the system must move left.

At point 3 the system is moving back toward the left, and its velocity is still increasing. Although the system must cross the x-axis vertically,[*] no such restriction applies to the y-axis, and we can find our point of maximum velocity (largest y) on either side of the y-axis or indeed right on it. Point 4 is our point of greatest speed and comes before we reach the y-axis. At point 5 the system is far to the left and has slowed down considerably, and by point 6 it has stopped for an instant before falling back. Again the path crosses the x-axis at a right angle. At point 7 the system is moving rightward and still picking up speed, while point 8 corresponds

---

[*]   As the velocity changes from positive to negative, the instantaneous position doesn't change, so the path in the phase plane must be vertical.

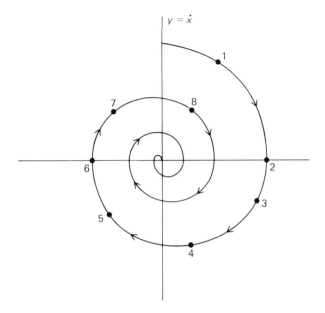

Figure 10.3 *A spiral approach to the origin.*

to point 1, except that both the displacement (x) and the velocity (y) are smaller, and there is hope that the system will spiral in toward the origin and eternal rest. In fact, it may be shown that system paths cannot cross each other, so it is pretty certain that things are going to end up at zero.

EIGHT TYPES OF BEHAVIOR

There are eight general classes of behavior of nonlinear systems in the vicinity of a singular point. They are illustrated in Figure 10.4(a) through (g). The first of these is a stable node, which is the behavior of an overdamped second-order system. If the system starts out with zero velocity (along the x-axis), it approaches the singular point without overshooting it. Only if the initial velocity is large will the system be carried beyond the stable point and then return; but note that since in every case the system must come to zero velocity in order to turn around, there is at most one excursion past the singular point before the system coasts in smoothly to a stop. Observe the dotted line. Its slope will depend on the characteristics of the system, but in no case will a path cross it. Figure 10.4(b) is a stable focus, which we have already discussed in Figure 10.2. It represents the same system as Figure 10.4(a) but is underdamped, leading to oscillatory behavior.

Figure 10.4(c) represents an unstable node. Again a dividing line separates the plane into two parts, but in this case the system runs off to infinity rather than settling down at the singular point. Figure 10.4(d) shows the same runaway behavior but for an oscillatory case in which the oscillations grow ever larger until a real life system would destroy itself. Figure 10.4(e) represents a case midway between the stable and the unstable focus, in which oscillations neither grow nor decay but maintain constant amplitude. It is called a center, and it is found in nature only in systems with zero damping.

The saddle point is an interesting phenomenon. It represents an unstable point that exerts a repulsive force on the system. If the system has a large displacement and relatively small velocity (the regions near the positive and negative x-axis), then the repulsive force will bring the system to a stop and turn it around to retreat in the direction from which it originally came. If the velocity is higher (the regions near the positive and negative y-axis), then the system will be moving fast enough to force its way past the singular point, but once past, the repulsion that had been slowing the system down now accelerates it, and it moves off with ever-increasing velocity.

All of the above behaviors can be observed in linear or nonlinear systems, but the next two occur only in nonlinear ones. They are called limit cycles. In a stable limit cycle, when the system is displaced from its stable cycle, it tends to return to it. You might imagine a marble rolling around in a circular trough. With amplitudes of oscillation less than that represented by the cycle, we have negative damping, and the oscillations grow in amplitude. Outside the limit cycle we have positive damping, and energy is withdrawn from the system, perhaps by friction, and the oscillations decay until we have just the right size again and the forces removing energy from the system just balance the forces putting in energy and we have, in effect, zero damping.

The unstable limit cycle, as its name implies, always diverges from the circular pathway. Inside the cycle, damping is positive and the system decays to rest at the singular point. Outside, damping is negative and the system rushes off to infinity.

Limit cycles can be nested inside each other to any depth imaginable, but a moment's thought should convince you that, reading outward from the singular point, they must be alternately stable and unstable (or vice versa). One may have several singular points along the x-axis (more than one makes for a lousy servo-mechanism), and again they must be alternately stable and unstable.

For a servo the location of the singular point moves as the input signal commands, varying output. Usually for simple systems the type of singular point does not change as it moves along the x-axis, but we can imagine an x-axis made up of patches of swamp (with high damping) and desert (with low) that might change a stable node to a stable focus or even a center or an unstable focus.

(Those not interested in mathematics may skip the rest of this section with relatively small loss.)

We can organize our understanding of the behaviors of linear systems in an interesting fashion. Consider again the second-order linear differential equation

$$\ddot{x} + r\dot{x} + sx = 0.$$

The general solution of this equation is given by

$$x = A\, e^{\lambda_1 t} + B\, e^{\lambda_2 t},$$

where λ_1 and λ_2 are the solutions of the equation

$$\lambda^2 + r\lambda + s = 0.$$

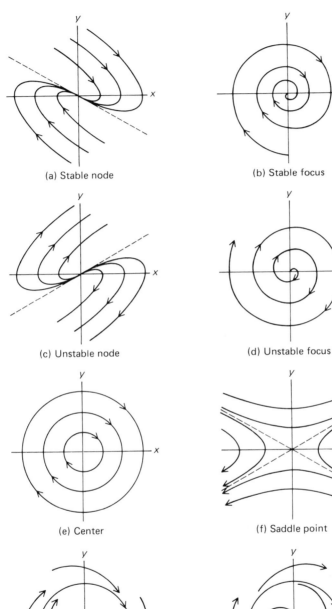
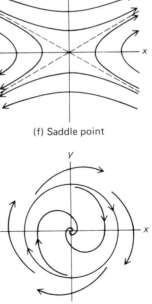

(a) Stable node

(b) Stable focus

(c) Unstable node

(d) Unstable focus

(e) Center

(f) Saddle point

(g) Stable limit cycle

(h) Unstable limit cycle

Figure 10.4 *The eight general forms of behavior of systems near a singular point.*

These solutions are

$$\lambda_1 = \frac{-r + \sqrt{r^2 - 4s}}{2},$$

$$\lambda_2 = \frac{-r - \sqrt{r^2 - 4s}}{2}.$$

The sign of the term under the radical $(r^2 - 4s)$ will determine whether the root is complex or real. A real root represents exponential decay or buildup (depending on the sign), whereas a complex root implies oscillation. Plot in the r–s plane the equation

$$r^2 = 4s.$$

That parabola, together with the r-axis and the positive s-axis, divides the world into five regions plus two lines (the parabola and the positive s-axis), as shown in Figure 10.5.

Inside the parabola r^2 is less than $4s$, so we have oscillation. On the parabola the oscillation is critically damped, and outside it is overdamped. In the right half plane, above the s-axis, r—the damping term—is positive, and the system ends up at the singular point. Below the s-axis the damping is negative, and the system diverges to infinity. On the s-axis damping is zero, and we find the centers. To the left of the r-axis we have s negative. That means that there is a force pushing the system away from the singular point, and this gives us saddle-point behaviors.

BANG-BANG SERVO REVISITED

In a bang-bang servo the motor is full on clockwise or full on counterclockwise. Consider the situation when the system is to the left of the singular point $(x < 0)$.

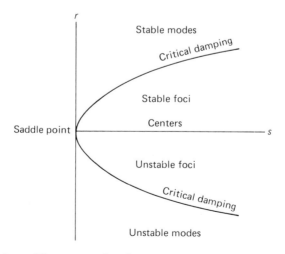

Figure 10.5 *Behaviors of linear second-order systems.*

The equation of motion is

$$I\ddot{\Theta} + f\dot{\Theta} - T = 0 \,.$$

Suppose for a moment that damping is not present ($f = 0$). Then the angular acceleration ($\ddot{\Theta}$) would be equal to a constant (T/I) and for constant acceleration we have the angular velocity ω, given by

$$\omega = kt \,,$$

where $k = T/I$, a linear function of time. And the angular position Θ would be given by

$$\Theta = \frac{1}{2} kt^2 \,.$$

If we want to plot ω versus Θ in the phase plane, we find that writing

$$t = \frac{\omega}{k}$$

and substituting, we have

$$\Theta = \frac{1}{2} \frac{\omega^2}{k} \,,$$

which is a parabola. (See Figure 10.6.)

   If we introduce damping by letting f be nonzero, we are going to follow a curve inside the zero damping parabola, because the damping force will tend to keep the system from accelerating quite as much. The dotted line in Figure 10.6 shows one such path with damping included. The exact shape of this path is not

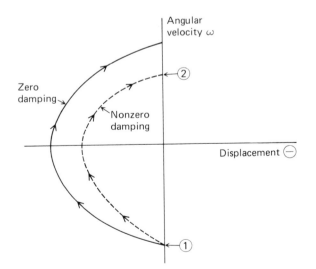

Figure 10.6 *The path of a bang-bang servo in the left half-phase plane.*

critical to our discussion, although it can be derived mathematically if required or even graphically when that seems desirable. What we need to notice about this path is that if we start out with zero displacement and large negative velocity (point 1), we will end up at zero displacement again (point 2) with a velocity of smaller magnitude than the one with which we began.

Note that so far we are talking only about the left half plane. Of course, everything is symmetric in the right half plane, and we see that a bang-bang servo does approach the singular point (see Figure 10.7), because on each return to zero displacement the velocity is less than the previous time. But sometimes the system doesn't quite come to rest. There is a small stable limit cycle close to the singular point. This can be caused by backlash in gears or quantization noise in the position sensor or by a number of other nonlinearities. This phenomenon is common enough to have several names. It is called "dither," "chatter," and "hunting." We will come back to this a bit later.

OPTIMUM CONTROL

Suppose we are off to the left of the singular point, approaching it from a great distance away at a constant speed. There comes a moment when we are just X feet away from the origin when, if we turn on the motor full force to the left, we will decelerate rapidly and arrive at the origin with exactly zero velocity. In slowing down like this, the motor will be aided by any friction in the system. Now at *whatever* speed we may be traveling, approaching the origin, there is an exact distance X where, by throwing on the motor full tilt away from the origin, we will come to a complete halt just as we reach the origin. Figure 10.8 shows the locus of such points as a function of the velocity for a hypothetical system. The locus is drawn in the phase plane, of course, since that is the plane of distance and velocity.

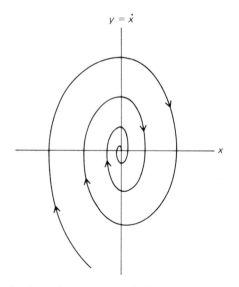

Figure 10.7 *Behavior of a bang-bang servo with damping shown in the phase plane.*

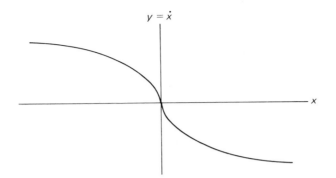

Figure 10.8 *Locus of critical stopping distances in the phase plane for a hypothetical bang-bang servo. This is called the "switching curve."*

If our system is anywhere along this locus of "stopping points," then we should apply full motor force (in the correct direction) to come to rest at the origin as fast as possible. As fast as possible? Yes! If we applied *less* than full force, we would overshoot (and waste time having to retrace our steps), and we can't apply *more* than full force. QED. Suppose we are not on the magic locus? Then apply full force to the motor to get to that curve as quickly as possible. If we are to the left of the locus, moving to the right, apply full motor force to the right until we reach the locus, and then throw the motor into reverse. If we are already past the locus still moving to the right, we are bound to overshoot the origin if we haven't already. So full force to the left will bring us to a stop as soon as possible and then back to the left until we reach the locus once again. Figure 10.9 shows some possible paths. If

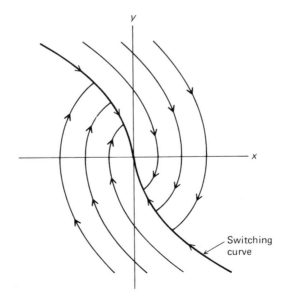

Figure 10.9 *Paths approaching the switching curve.*

you are below the so-called "switching curve," you apply full motor power to the right. If you are above, the power is to the left. When you reach the locus of critical stopping distances, you switch the sign of the motor power. That's why it's called the switching curve.

Since the system is getting to the singular point in as short a time as possible,[*] this is called "optimum control." In real life the switching curve is fairly nonlinear, and before cheap digital computers came along, optimum control was only of academic interest, since finding an analog circuit to switch accurately and reliably was quite difficult. But with microcomputers and table-look-up, optimum control is now available for use by anybody with the price of a CPU chip. Let's take our servo hardware from Chapter 8 and first measure the switching curve and then close the loop.

Exercise 10.1: Measuring the Switching Curve

Given our hardware, perhaps the most convenient way to measure the switching curve is as follows:

1. Turn the motor on full force clockwise for N revolutions ($N = 5, 10, 15, \ldots$).
2. On the Nth revolution, measure the time required to complete the full revolution. This gives you an estimate of the speed.
3. Turn the motor on full force counterclockwise, and count the number of revolutions before the system actually reverses direction. That is your measure of the stopping distance of the system at that speed.
4. Printout speed and stopping distance.
5. Next N.

You might check a few points going in the other direction to see if the system is symmetric or not. Plot up the stopping distance as a function of rotation period. From this you should be able to interpolate to get a table of "critical rotation periods" for each integer value of stopping distance from one revolution out to perhaps 40 or 50 revolutions.

To make your servo display optimum performance, you can use an algorithm similar to this one:

1. Observe how far you are from the command point. Call this distance D.
2. Look up the "critical rotation period" for this distance D. Call it V.
3. If the rotation period of the system as measured for the most recent rotation is longer than the critical rotation period, the speed of the system is less than the critical speed, so keep on accelerating full force *toward* the command point. Otherwise, accelerate full force *away* from the command point.

---

[*]   We haven't *proved* that, but it *is* true.

This will converge toward the command point, and then, because of the quantized nature of the distance measure, you may get a residual dither. There are two basic ways to get rid of this dither. One is to declare that plus or minus N revolutions is "close enough for government work," and whenever you are within that "dead band," you just shut off the motor entirely. Depending on the system, you may be able to make N as small as one or two and still eliminate all hunting behavior.

The other method is more elegant. It combines the race-for-home nature of optimum control with the smoother action of proportional control. That method says that when the distance error is greater than P, we use optimum control; less than P revolutions away, we use proportional control. A P around 10 sounds like a good switchover value. We haven't actually tried that.

Exercise 10.2: Closing the Loop

Now that you have your carefully calibrated optimum control system working, make the command input switch between 64 and 192 with a 10-second dwell at each value, and observe that the system follows the square-wave input with little or no overshoot. Then put on the large gear we were using to increase inertia. What happens? Lots of overshoot? Take off the large gear and try the fan. Very jerky behavior as the system keeps wandering either side of the switching curve? The answer to both questions should be yes. What we have done is build a system that, like the dinosaurs, can't cope with changes in its environment. If the power line surges and the motor runs a little faster, or if the gears and bearings get gummy and sticky, the system is thrown out of kilter and is no longer optimum. Now, I don't know about your mother, but mine didn't raise her little boy to spend all his life sitting around tuning up an optimum control system. Can't something be done? Isn't there some way to adapt to changes in the environment?

ADAPTIVE CONTROL

Suppose we discover that the system is consistently overshooting the command point. That would indicate that either inertia has increased or damping or motor torque has decreased. In either event, what we need to do is to start applying the "brakes" a little earlier. Suppose the input is still a square wave. We sense the change in the command point, apply full force in the proper direction, reach what used to be the switching curve at distance D from the command point, and turn on full force in the other direction. Instead of coming to a stop after D revolutions, as we expected, we come to a stop after D' revolutions. But in so doing, we have traversed exactly along the *new* optimal switching curve. At each revolution of the shaft, as we traverse this curve, we can measure the period of rotation, and when we finally come to a stop, we will know how many revolutions we were away from a stop when we made that measurement.

Suppose we have been operating from a table similar to Table 10.1. This table says that if you are, for example, 4 revolutions away from the command point and

Table 10.1 Critical Period versus Numbered Revolutions
Away from the Command Point.

Revolutions away from the singular point	Critical period of revolution, in seconds
0	∞
1	.55
2	.38
3	.25
4	.2
5	.183
6	.170

your period of revolution is greater than .2 seconds (you are turning at less than 5 rps), you should keep on accelerating toward the command point. If, however, your revolution period is less than .2 seconds (you are turning faster than 5 revolutions per second), you should be decelerating as hard as you can.

Now you come driving full force toward the command point, strike the switching curve N revolutions away from the origin, and reverse the motor. You observe carefully how long it takes you to complete the next revolution. Let that time be equal to P_o—the observed period. By looking in the switching curve table entry for $N - 1$ revolutions out from the origin, you can discover how long it should have taken you to complete this revolution if you are to reach the origin with zero velocity. That's what the switching curve *is*. Call this value P_e—the expected period.

Now compare P_o and P_e. If P_o is greater than P_e, your observed period is too long. First of all, that means that you are below the switching curve and should turn the motor to accelerating the system. That is the short-term response of the system. Adaptation has to do with the long-term behavior. You are turning too slowly (the braking is more effective than you expected), and you are going to come to a stop too soon. That is, you are going to undershoot the origin, and you could have been going faster (had a smaller rotation period) when you applied the brakes—or stating it another way, you could have waited longer before beginning to slow down. All of this says that the inertia of the system has decreased or the motor is somehow more powerful than it used to be. In this case, you want to *decrease* the number stored in the switching curve table at distance N, because decreasing the period means increasing the rotational speed permitted.

Suppose, on the other hand, the motor is a bit weaker, or the inertia has increased, or somebody has oiled the bearings reducing the friction. In any of these cases your braking is going to be less effective than you expected, and when you compare P_o with P_e, you will find that the shaft is turning faster than it ought to be, and the period of rotation observed is smaller than the period of rotation expected ($P_o < P_e$). You are going to overshoot the origin. Now you should decrease

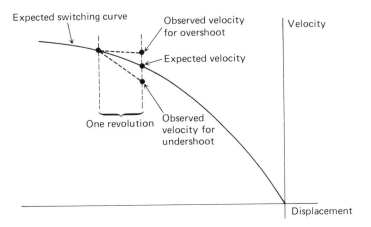

Figure 10.10 *Observed velocity and expected velocity after one revolution.*

the speed allowed at distance N by increasing the critical period stored in the Nth entry of the switching table. Figure 10.10 shows these two cases. Remember that we are plotting velocity, which is the reciprocal of the period.

When $P_o < P_e$ (overshoot), we should increase the entry in the switching table at distance N. When $P_o > P_e$ (undershoot), we should decrease that entry. We can do this easily by adding to P_N, a quantity proportional to

$$P_e - P_o \qquad \text{observed at} \qquad N - 1.$$

If we add in the total difference, we may be introducing problems due to transient phenomena or to quantization noise. On the other hand, if we take only a small fraction of the difference as a correction, it will take a very long time for our system to adapt to changes in the outside world.

Exercise 10.3: Optimal Control

Rewrite the bang-bang control program (Exercise 9.1) to adapt to changes in the system by adding in a correction to the switching table entries, as discussed above. If we let T_N be the time at which we are N revolutions away from the origin and T_{N-1} be the time at which we are $N - 1$ revolutions away, then

$$P_o = T_{N-1} - T_N.$$

The expected period when we reach $N - 1$ revolutions away will be called

$$P_{N-1},$$

and we will correct P_N by the equation

$$P_N = P_N + k(P_{N-1} + P_o).$$

Try several values of k. For example, $k = 1/2, 1/4, 1/8, 1/16$. How fast does the system adapt in each case? That is, how many steps of the square wave before the overshoot is negligible? How stable is the behavior?

Remember that in real life sudden changes in a system are less to be worried about than slow progressive changes, so in real life we would opt for somewhat slower adaptation to promote stability and smooth performance.

SOPHISTICATED ADAPTATION

In a real sense, adaptive optimal control provides a second feedback loop around the original feedback control system: an outer loop that controls the behavioral constants of the inner loop. What we have described above is a very primitive control system that will adjust the switching curve of the primary system, much as a first-order system adjusts its outputs to agree with its inputs.

As you might expect, much more sophisticated adaptive algorithms have been proposed and used. We talked about an adaptive loop that caused the inner loop to approach optimal performance exponentially, but surely we could do better than that. Perhaps we could make the adaptive loop itself behave in "optimal" fashion, making large, swift, dexterous changes in the parameters of the inner loop so that it approached optimality as rapidly as possible. And if we did that, couldn't we add a third loop that adapted the adaptive loop? And so on, ad infinitum. For our purposes it is sufficient that you understand the basics of adaptation and realize that infinite regression is conceivable, if not necessarily practical.

11 The Lunar Lander

The LEM is descending rapidly, fuel almost gone. Desperately the pilot clenches his controls knowing he has only one chance to fire his retro rockets and bring the vehicle to a halt just as it reaches the surface. His radar set ticks off the altitude: 1,000 meters, 900 meters, 800—Fire! Flame lances out and the lander is obscured in a cloud of dust kicked up by the rocket exhaust.

How can we go about making a model of the above situation that will have some aspects of realism? Of course, we could do it all *inside* a computer and only print out the numbers, but it would be much more fun to have a model Lunar Excursion Module lowered from the ceiling on a string. What do we need to do? We need a means of controlling the altitude of the module and a means of measuring that altitude. Briefly, we can control position with a DC motor like the servo of Chapter 8, with a stepping motor, or with jet propulsion. We can measure position with a potentiometer, a photodisk, switches, or photocells, or by sonar. We will look at each of these.

SERVO MOTOR

The most obvious way to control position is with a servo system, such as we developed in Chapter 8. For smoothness of operation and because our time scale will be long with respect to the distances we have to travel, a linear proportional servo will probably be the best. In that system, we used a 3/16 inch shaft, which had a circumference of 3/16 · π or .589 inch, or something under .6 inch. That means that a string wrapped around the shaft would be let out .6 inch for each revolution of the shaft. We could use this to measure the altitude of the LEM directly. Starting with the LEM on the ground, the initialization procedures could raise it a known number of turns. For example, 100 turns would raise it 60 inches or five feet. We could easily halve the quantum of height by putting another notch in the photocell masking gear and getting a detection of each .3 inch change in altitude. We could, if it seemed necessary, even replace the photocells and gear with a binary-encoded photodisk and measure down to a small fraction of a turn. But this system relies on the computer's keeping an accurate count of the total number of revolutions that have taken place. Any time somebody has to keep a count, there is an opportunity for error. One should generally avoid "counts" whenever possible.

We could avoid counting by gearing a photodisk down by 100:1 from the output shaft. We could replace the photodisk by a potentiometer (also suitably geared down) and an A to D converter, and there are various ways of direct distance measurement we will look at in just a minute.

STEPPING MOTOR

The next possibility is to replace the servo motor with its continuous control of position by a stepping motor that has discrete positions. Basically, a stepping motor is an electromechanical device that, upon receipt of the proper signal or signals, changes the angle of the output shaft from Θ to $\Theta + \delta$, where δ may be as small as .1° or as large as 90°. Bidirectional stepping motors require fairly complex signals to cause them to move through a complete step. There are a couple of articles in *Byte* that provide a good introduction to steppers. ("A Stepping Motor Primer," Paul Giacomo, *Byte,* February and March 1979, Vol. 4, nos. 2 and 3.)

Steppers vary in the number of control lines they have. A three-line or three-phase stepper has lines A, B, and C plus a common line. To cause it to turn clockwise, you will have to go through the following sequence of actions.

Assume phase A is energized.

1. Energize (turn on) phase B.
2. Turn off phase A.
3. Turn on phase C.
4. Turn off phase B.
5. Turn on phase A.
6. Turn off phase C.

To turn counterclockwise, you need to take the following actions.

1. Turn on C.
2. Turn off A.
3. Turn on B.
4. Turn off C.
5. Turn on A.
6. Turn off B.

Drive circuits for each control line can be as simple as that shown in Figure 11.1 or considerably more complicated, depending on the motor. Stepping rates up to several hundred per second and down to DC are available.

ROCKETS

Of great intuitive appeal would be actual operation of a rocket motor to generate downward thrust and thus control acceleration, velocity, and position. Not wishing to go into competition with NASA or to stir up the ire of the local fire department, let us hasten to say that we don't mean real burning-type rockets.

As of the time of this writing, Edmund Scientific was selling solenoid-controlled valves for air or water for less than a dollar apiece. Suppose you bought about eight of these and arranged them on a wheeled cart, all pointing out of the back end. We connect the other side of the valves together and to a paint sprayer compressor (or to the spare tire of an automobile) via a long hose. By connecting the solenoids (through drivers) to an output port, you could vary the thrust from zero to 8 in steps of one unit. If you have a tolerant mate, mother, or lab instructor, you will get a lot more thrust if you use water rather than air as a working fluid. Watch for short circuits, though, for water is a good conductor. If we remember correctly, the sorcerer's apprentice found that a magic broom was good for sweeping away the water delivered by the magic pump he didn't know how to stop.

An inclined plane can simulate the weak gravitational field of the moon, and by varying the angle, you can get the force due to gravity pulling the cart downward along the plane to be less than the maximum thrust available from your rocket motor. To be perfectly honest, we have not tried this, but it sounds like fun.

DIRECT MEASUREMENT OF POSITION

Whatever method of position control we choose, we are still going to need to measure the position—and preferably directly, not by counting.

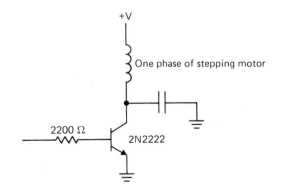

Figure 11.1 *Drive circuit for one phase of a stepping motor.*

One scheme might be to run the LEM on a vertical rod or track and place near that track a lot of microswitches, so placed that the LEM will close one at a time. Which one will depend on the altitude.

Putting one switch every inch, we get about 64 switches in 5 feet 4 inches of height. We can connect the switches in 8 banks of 8 each, as indicated in Figure 11.2, and by scanning across port A (values 1, 2, 4, 8, 10, 20, 40, 80), we can look for a one in port B to find out which switch is closed.

We can replace microswitches with photocells or with magnetically operated reed switches (the magnet would be mounted on the LEM) if we want to get away from physical contact.

A very much more elegant solution is to use sonar as a substitute for radar and to measure the distance between a sound source (loudspeaker) and a sound detector (microphone) by measuring how long the sound takes to travel between them. The circuits presented here are due to Dr. Nico Spinelli, who developed them in order to build his own inexpensive graph digitizer.

At one time, Poly Paks[*] was selling ultrasonic transducers for a couple of bucks each. The advantage of an ultrasonic transducer is that it is immune to room noise.

A spark released in the air generates a good deal of ultrasonic energy. We put the detector in the LEM and the spark generator on the ground below it. This isn't really sonar, which relies on reflected sound, but it gives us a lot better range and is just as accurate. Circuits for these devices are shown in Figure 11.3. If the ultrasonic transducers are not available, you might persuade a camera repair shop to sell you a "distance sensing device" from a Polaroid SX-70 self-focusing camera.[†] It's basically the same thing. (Ask them to give you some instructions on which pin is which.)

Sound travels about 1 foot per millisecond in air, so measurements to an accuracy of ±1 microseconds would represent an error of about 1/100 of an inch, quite close enough, we would imagine, for government work.

Set up a timer and start it. Output a one to trigger off the spark, and then watch for the transducer to catch the sound wave. A distance of three feet will mean a delay of 3 milliseconds. Therefore an 8-bit counter should count at about one count per 12 microseconds to make a count of 255 correspond to a 3-foot distance. More bits in the counter and a higher counting rate will give a greater accuracy of position. Our spark generator and detector seemed to work quite reliably out to about 3 feet and became erratic beyond this distance.

VELOCITY MEASUREMENT

In addition to position, the pilot for the lunar lander would like to know how fast he is descending.

---

[*]   Poly Paks, P.O. Box 942, South Lynnfield, MA 01940.

[†]   Polaroid now puts these out as an experimenter's kit. Write to Polaroid Corp., Ultrasonic Ranging Marketing, 20 Ames St., Cambridge, MA 02139.

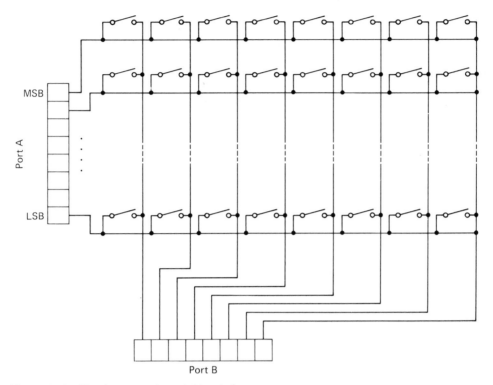

Figure 11.2 *Matrix connection of 64 switches to two ports.*

We can infer the velocity from the time rate of change of the position. With the servo of Chapter 8, we measure the time required to complete a revolution and invert this number by division or table look-up to get revolutions per second.

With the sonar system, we can send out a pulse every N milliseconds (where N is greater than the longest possible traversal time) and measure the difference between two successive positions as a velocity (the distance moved in N milliseconds). There are devices that measure angular velocity directly. They are called tachometers. Real tachometers are expensive, but you can make one fairly inexpensively by using a cheap DC motor as a generator. Gear the motor up 4 or 5 to 1 from the output shaft so that it turns rapidly. Ground one lead and connect the other to an A to D converter. You'll have to calibrate the thing, but once it is calibrated, it will be consistent in its readings.

EQUATIONS OF MOTION

Our lunar lander is confined to one dimension, although you could think about a three-dimensional model if you wanted. The forces acting in a vertical direction are two: gravitation pulling downward and the reaction force generated by the rocket motor pushing up. Let us assume that the rocket motor is burning with a thrust T, where the pilot can adjust T from zero to some maximum value. At thrust T, we are consuming some number of pounds of fuel per second. For simplicity, assume a linear relation between thrust and fuel consumption, and further let the constant of proportionality be one. So once every N milliseconds we will subtract T from the "amount of fuel remaining $= F$." If A goes negative, we are out of fuel and begin to fall with ever-increasing velocity until we reach the surface. We can adjust the maximum duration of a "burn" by adjusting the initial value stored in F. One probably should plan on double-precision arithmetic for F. Given a sonar pulse repetition frequency (called PRF) of 10 Hz and consequently a major cycle every .1 second, even a thrust of one unit will exhaust a single-precision register in less than 25 seconds.

The downward acceleration due to lunar gravity is approximately 5 feet per second per second, or .165 of the surface gravity of the earth. Let us assume our rocket motor can generate acceleration of 0, 1, 2, . . . , 32 feet per second per second—or "zero to one gee," as we astronauts say. The rocket acceleration will be upwards, the gravity will be down. So each major cycle we will compute first the net acceleration:

$$a = T - 5. \tag{11.1}$$

We can compute the velocity by summing (or integrating) acceleration, so the new velocity will be

$$v' = v + a, \tag{11.2}$$

and similarly the position will be given by

$$x' = x + v, \tag{11.3}$$

where X is the altitude above the surface in "feet."

Vertical position was measured using the spark gap sonar of Figure 11.3. This position was compared each major cycle with the desired position computed from Equation 11.3 and the servo motor driven in a direction to reduce the error with a force proportional to the magnitude of the error. We didn't use the photocell position detectors on the servo at all. We put the servo board on a table and hung the "lander" over the edge on a pulley. "Coil cord" was constructed by wrapping wire in a coil around a pencil. We used two pairs of wires. One pair energized a red-painted flashlight bulb to simulate the firing of the rocket motors. The other pair went to the primary of the spark transformer. We placed the ultrasonic detector on the floor under the lander vehicle with wires coming up to our control box. Our lander consisted of a tin can, but more realism would be obtained from a plastic model purchased at a hobby or toy store.

INTERFACE WITH THE PILOT

Depending on how elaborate the information is that you choose to give the pilot, he will take a greater or lesser time to learn how to handle the LEM. You might use seven-segment displays to tell him the altitude and vertical velocity and amount of fuel remaining. You might tell him only the fuel remaining and let him judge the velocity and altitude from observation of the model.

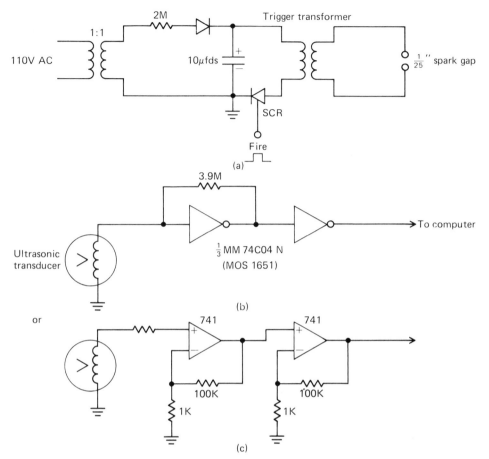

Figure 11.3 *Circuits for spark generator and detector. Note that you must use a C series inverter in (b). A 7404 or 74LS04 won't work here.*

We provided the pilot with a potentiometer that controlled thrust. Fully counterclockwise was zero thrust, and fully clockwise was maximum thrust. An A to D converter enabled the computer to read this input.

Our machine has six digits of display built into it. We used standard display driving routines[*] to display altitude, thrust, and tons of fuel remaining, two hex digits each. Some of our students have become quite proficient at handling the system, and we may end up recommending them to NASA as future pilots.

Exercise 11.1: Lunar Excursion Module

Select an approach from the above discussion and implement and program it.

---

[*] See Caxton C. Foster, *Programming a Microcomputer: 6502*, Addison-Wesley, Reading, MA 1978.

12 Communication over Restricted Pathways

In this chapter we are going to consider the problem of passing information from a stationary (more or less) computer to a remote and mobile peripheral device. You might want to think of a robotlike mechanism scuttling about doing the bidding of the supercomputer in the basement, or you might want to be a bit more realistic and consider model railroad trains and radio-controlled model airplanes.

Both model railroads and radio-controlled model airplanes offer great possibilities for the application of microcomputers for control purposes. These models reproduce in miniature many of the problems inherent in larger systems at considerably reduced expense. Since both require a number of different signals to be sent over one pathway, they offer an excuse for talking about multiplexing and about how one can represent information.

Military interest in remote-piloted vehicles (RPVs) is due, in part, to the low cost of the system and to the fact that a pilot does not have to be retrieved if the ship is shot down over hostile territory. But even though nobody will ever admit it, part of the interest is probably due to the fact that model planes are fun. Typical systems use four or more separate control signals (called channels) coupling the hand-held transmitter to the airplane up in the sky. These channels are usually: motor control for speed, ailerons for banking, elevators for climbs and dives, and rudder for turns. Fancy systems offer up to eight independent channels to control flaps, retractable landing gear, lights, bomb releases, and many other functions in addition to the basic four.

The pilot (what else can we call him?) stands on the ground with the transmitter in his hands, and by moving various knobs and levers, he causes the control surfaces of the plane to move back and forth in sympathy, and the plane to follow suit. The control loop is closed through the pilot's eyes and brain, where he compares the behavior of the plane with his desires or with a prescribed pattern of maneuvers that must be carried out exactly to win a prize.

One of the problems in our world is that there are too many people competing for the same resources. This affects model aviation by limiting the amount of the radio spectrum that can be used to control remote models. All told, there are about 12 frequencies that have been assigned for these purposes, and if a particular pilot used a different frequency for the control of each function, no more than one or two planes could be in the air at a single time. For races, one would like many planes up at one time, so each pilot is limited to using a single frequency, and he (or rather, the manufacturer of his radio system) must somehow cram all the information he wishes to transmit onto one frequency. Because computers can be used to aid in this process, and because the problem of remote control often comes up in computer application, we will look at various ways of conveying information from one spot to another. We will look first at how to convey one signal and then at how to convey several signals over a single pair of wires. Wired (as opposed to wireless) control won't be too convenient for model airplanes, but it will be ideal for model railroads, where the track can serve both to carry power and to control information. Now, we seldom want to make trains do other than go faster or slower; but in a large layout, we may want to control several engines at one time, and we would like to have a system whereby lever 5 controls the speed of engine 5, no matter where that engine is on the track.

SINGLE-CHANNEL CONTROL

We have one lever "here," and we wish to control the position of one control surface or the speed of one motor "over there" (see Figure 12.1). We measure the position of the lever and somehow send information about that position to the remote site where that information will be reconverted to a speed or a position.

Suppose we have a signal of whatever complexity that we wish to send from A to B. If A and B are both stationary, we can convert that signal to a voltage and impress that voltage onto a wire connecting A with B. There is some sort of voltage-sensitive device at B's end of the wire that converts the voltage back into some sort of useful event. He might have a power amplifier and a loudspeaker that will make the voltage into a sound wave, or he may use the voltage as a command input to a servo, which controls the outlet gates of a giant dam or whatever else he might think of. The ordinary local telephone works in this fashion, providing wired pathways between two remote but fixed points.

But what happens if one of the points is moving around a lot? Then we have to pass the information over a medium more elastic and flexible than copper wires. The usual way to do this is to establish a radio link between A and B. A has a transmitter that generates a wave of a particular frequency. B has a receiver tuned to that very frequency. Then if A causes the broadcast signal to vary in amplitude or phase or frequency or polarization, B can presumably detect these changes; and if A makes his changes in correspondence with the changes in some variable, then B can recover those changes and discover what value the variable has at any given instant in time.

Figure 12.1   *The transmission of information from a control stick to an actuator.*

There are four different schemes for encoding information in general use. They are called amplitude modulation (AM), frequency modulation (FM), pulse duration modulation (PDM), and pulse code modulation (PCM). We'll deal with each in turn.

AM

Suppose I have a radio wave oscillating one million times a second. Call this the carrier wave. Let there be a device called a "modulator" that accepts the carrier wave and the information wave form and generates a signal whose frequency is that of the carrier wave and whose amplitude is proportional to the magnitude of the information. See Figure 12.2. This device usually consists of a fast analog multiplier.

The reason for impressing the signal on a carrier rather than just sending out the original signal itself is that a number of signals can be impressed, each on its own carrier, each of which has a different frequency. We take the radio band from 500,000 Hz to 1,500,000 Hz and divide it into a number of separate carrier frequencies. Then, using filters with very narrow pass bands, we can "tune in" to one carrier or another and by appropriate signal processing (read "amplification and rectification" if you prefer those words), we can recover the original signal. Just the one signal to whose carrier we happen to be tuned. This is how the AM band of a radio works.

If only one signal is to be sent and wires can connect the source and destination, we don't need a carrier at all but can just put a voltage on the line that represents the information we wish to convey.

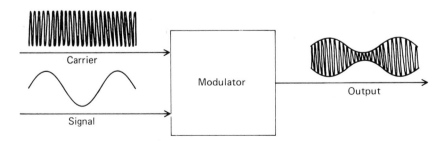

Figure 12.2   *Amplitude modulation.*

FM

In a frequency modulation system we will vary the frequency of the carrier slightly to represent various input values. For example, zero volts might be represented by the regular carrier frequency 1,000,000 Hz, minus one volt by 950,000 Hz, and plus one volt by 1,050,000 Hz. Figure 12.3 shows a greatly exaggerated picture of frequency modulation. This is the way FM radio stations work. Each has a separate carrier frequency in the range from 88 megahertz to 108 megahertz, and each is given a 150 kilohertz (± 75 kHz) band to use for its signal. FM is usually less noisy than AM, because lightning strikes and motors and the like can generate noise that will come in on top of an AM signal (as variations in amplitude) but won't change the frequency of a carrier very much, and hence when the frequency is measured rather than the amplitude, the noise disappears.

Frequency modulation is most easily accomplished by using an analog device called a "voltage-controlled oscillator," or VCO. At the receiving end, classical FM sets use a thing called a "discriminator" to change the frequency variations back into a voltage. Let's look and see how we might carry out FM communication between a pair of microcomputers. We will assume our signal is slowly varying, so we don't get into any problems with sampling or Nyquist frequencies. We will let the size of the number we wish to convey be mapped into the half period of the square wave we are going to transmit. If we have a repeating timer, we simply set up the timer so that it repeats continuously. On each output of the timer, we complement a flip-flop, so it sends zeros and ones alternately. When the command signal changes (or on a regular schedule if that is easier), we store the new value of the variable into the timer so the new half period will reflect that new value. If we don't have a repeating timer handy, the code of Figure 12.4 will do the trick. We connect the low-order bit of the output port LINE to the communication line between the computers, and then every time we increment the number stored there, the low-order bit changes from zero to one, or vice versa.

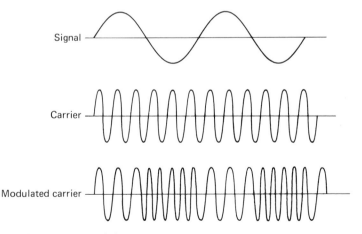

Figure 12.3 *Frequency modulation.*

```
BEGIN:    LDA        VALUE
LOOP1:    SUBIM      1
          BNA        LOOP1
          LDAIM      0
          OUTPUT     LINE
          LDA        VALUE
LOOP2:    SUBIM      1
          BNA        LOOP2
          LDAIM      1
          OUTPUT     LINE
          JMP        BEGIN
```

Figure 12.4 *A simple loop to generate a square wave whose half period is proportional to VALUE.*

At the receiving end, we are going to count not the interval between changes but how many of these changes occur in a fixed period of time. That is, we are going to measure the frequency of the signal. This way a stray random change due to noise will get swamped out by the true changes the transmitter is sending and not cause us any trouble. We can sit in a loop counting changes in the input and get interrupted by a timer at the end of one second. On the other hand, we can sit in a timing loop and get interrupted by a change in the input. Yet again, we can use a pair of sophisticated timers, one to count the one-second period and the other as an event timer to count the changes from zero to one. Figure 12.5 employs a mythical timer that works in four-millisecond steps, and the program counts how many times the input goes from zero to one (and back again) in one second. Note that

```
START:   LDAIM    250          Decimal 250 goes to a
         STA      TIMER        timer whose period is 4
                               milliseconds per count.

         LDAIM    0
         STA      COUNTER      Clear a counter.
WAIT1:   INPUT    SIGNAL
         BZA      WAIT1        Wait for signal to go to 1.
         LDA      COUNTER
         ADDIM    1            Add 1 to counter.
         STA      COUNTER
WAIT0:   INPUT    SIGNAL
         BNA      WAIT0        Wait for signal to go back to 0.
         LDA      TIMER
         BNA      WAIT1        If one second not over: loop.
```

Figure 12.5 *Code to count the number of times SIGNAL goes from 0 to 1 per second.*

coming out of Figure 12.5 we have a number that is proportional to one over the original number in VALUE in Figure 12.4. (Why?) This can be rectified by using the number found in Figure 12.5 as an index to a table that will hold the original numbers.

An interesting variation of frequency modulation is sometimes employed when only two numbers (zero and one) are to be sent. This is called "frequency shift keying," or FSK. A version of FSK is used in the KIM-1 to record information on noisy, unreliable cassette tapes with very good accuracy. The KIM produces one of two signal patterns, depending on whether you want to record a zero or a one. For a zero, it sends frequency f_1 for two time periods and then frequency f_2 for one time period. For a one, it sends f_1 for one time period and then f_2 for two periods. Using an analog discriminator, the input routine needs only to measure the relative durations of f_1 and f_2 to establish which pattern was encoded. You can change the length of the basic time period by a factor of six without confusing the receiver, which makes the system quite immune to noise and tape wow and flutter.

PDM

The third system to consider is called pulse duration modulation. We have already met it as a primitive form of digital to analog converter in Chapter 5. It is the scheme actually used by almost all model airplane radio control systems. In these systems, a pulse is sent whose width (or duration) varies from .5 to 1.5 milliseconds. One-millisecond pulses mean the control surface is to be placed in the neutral or center position. A pulse of .5 millisecond means right full rudder, and a pulse of 1.5 milliseconds means left full rudder. On another channel, the pulse durations might mean full speed or minimum speed or bank left or right or climb or dive. Pulse durations of less than the extremes imply control surface motion of smaller amounts, and more or less continuous control of the function can be achieved. The major advantage of PDM is that the pulse height carries no information, so weak signals don't contribute to errors. Only the duration matters.

Let us design a computerized encoder for a four-channel PDM control system. Once every 50th of a second, or once every 20 millisecond, we are going to send a string of four pulses from the transmitter to the receiver. We will leave the carrier frequency normally on and turn it off only for the duration of the pulses. We do it this way so that most of the time the receiver will be hearing our transmitter and will not be left open to listen for faint signals from some CBer or another model aviator in the next county. In other words, we are going to *amplitude-modulate* the carrier with pulses that carry information encoded by *pulse duration,* and we are going to divide time up into separate "slots" or divisions, one for each pulse, so we will be doing "time-division multiplexing" (see Figure 12.6). The first pulse will start at time 0, the second pulse at 3 milliseconds, the third at 6 milliseconds, and the fourth at 9 milliseconds. The fourth pulse will be all over by 10½ milliseconds at the latest, and there is then a pause of at least 9½ milliseconds, called the "re-synching pause," which the receiver uses so it can keep straight which channel is which. The set of pulses and the pause together are called a frame, and we are go-

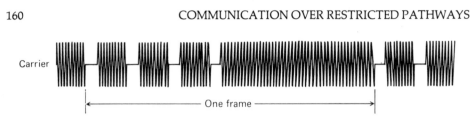

Carrier

|← ————————— One frame ————————— →|

Figure 12.6 *One frame of a four-channel control system.*

ing to have a frame rate of 50 frames per second. What does that tell you about the maximum frequency that may be present in an input signal? Given that humans are going to be generating these frequencies by moving their fingers around, do you think this is likely to be a problem? What would you do if it were?

The first thing to do is to start a timer going that will time out after 3 milliseconds. As soon as we have that running, we start the pulse for channel 1. An 8-bit number representing the first channel of information varies from 0 to 255. We can divide the value to be transmitted in half, giving a range of 0–127, add 64 to it, translating to a range of 64 to 191, and let each count stand for 8 microseconds. We can load the translated count into a register and count down to zero with an 8-microsecond loop like:

```
              LDAIM       0
              OUTPUT      TRANSMITTER        Turn off the transmitter.
              LDA         VALUE              A number between 64 and
                                             191.
DELAY:        NOP                            Insert enough NOPs to
              NOP                            bring the loop time to 8
              SUBIM       1                  microseconds.
              BNA         DELAY
              LDAIM       1
              OUTPUT      TRANSMITTER        Turn transmitter on.
```

Or we could use a timer similar to the ones discussed in Chapter 2.

When our channel 1 pulse is over, we wait for the 3-millisecond timer to time out. Then we start another 3-millisecond time interval and also start the pulse for channel 2. We repeat the process for channel 3, but for channel 4 we start a timer that will last 11 milliseconds, and when that timer times out, we begin another frame. During the last 9 or 10 milliseconds of the resynching pause, our computer will be free to compute whatever we need to compute, just so long as we get back to start the next frame.

At the receiver we can do things a little differently. Whenever we receive the beginning of a pulse, we will start (or restart) a 7-millisecond timer. That's halfway between 3 and 11 milliseconds, and if the receiver and transmitter clocks don't run at quite the same speed, that is the value that gives the most margin for error. Whenever that timer times out, we know that we are in a resynching pause, and the next pulse we detect (the next time the carrier goes off) will be the beginning of a new frame. We let the timer interrupt the program and force transfer of control to the first line of code in Figure 12.7.

```
CHANONE:    INPUT     CARRIER     Test to see if carrier is on or off.
            BNA       CHANONE     Wait for it to go to zero.
            LDAIM     CONST       Get an appropriate constant
            STA       TIMER       to run timer for 7 milliseconds.
            LDAIM     1
            OUTPUT    SERVO1      Send 1 to SERVO1.
   WONE:    INPUT     CARRIER     Test for end of first "pulse."
            BZA       WONE        Wait for carrier to go to one.
            LDAIM     0
            OUTPUT    SERVO1      Turn off signal to SERVO1.
CHANTWO:    LDA       CARRIER     Wait here for beginning
            BNA       CHANTWO     of pulse 2.
               .
               .
               .
            OUTPUT    SERVO4      End of pulse 4.
    IDLE:   INPUT     TIMER       Wait for signal from timer
            BNA       IDLE        to take us back to CHANONE.
            JMP       CHANONE
```

Figure 12.7 *The receiver program for a four-channel system.*

Model airplane servos are already designed to accept a variable width pulse and turn the output shaft proportionally as the pulse grows longer or shorter. We assume in Figure 12.7 that we have a carrier detector that is either zero or one connected to the input port (CARRIER) and that we have four separate output ports, one going to each servo. Doing the receiver with a computer is something of an overkill, since aside from the radio receiver and carrier detector parts, the rest can be done with a couple of MSI chips at a far lower cost. But let's try to justify the computer on safety grounds.

At the beginning of the program, where you wait for the start of pulse 1, let's put in a counter that gets initialized and then counts out after 1000 milliseconds if no new frame has begun. That's time for 50 frames. If no new frame is begun in that period of time, the transmitter must be off the air, the receiver must be broken, or the plane must be out of range of the transmitter. We would like to try to recover our plane if we can. Throttle the motor back as much as possible, put ailerons and elevator in neutral, and insert a gentle left (or right) turn on the rudder. The plane should begin to coast down toward the earth in a large spiral. If you have flaps and landing gear, deploy these as well. And keep listening for the receiver; maybe by some miracle it will come back on.

One can imagine another use for an on-board computer in a model plane. Some of the contests involve a very complex, high-speed series of maneuvers that must be executed with consummate skill. Clever Charles has an on-board computer with the series of maneuvers stored as a program that can be called into play whenever he pushes lever 8 all the way home. He gets his plane flying straight and level right past the judging stand and pulses the secret lever. With computerlike precision, his plane executes the pattern at blinding speed. With snarls of envy, the other contestants turn away in dejection as the crowd roars its approval. Right? Now you should know computers better than that. Somewhere about halfway through the pattern, there will be an undetected bug in the program and the vertical 8 will be converted into a vertical figure 9—right smack into the tarmac. Still it's an interesting idea.

PCM

Pulse code modulation scarcely needs discussion in this book. Instead of sending an analog signal, we send a pattern of zeros and ones ("no pulses" and "pulses") that represents the analog information in digital form. Each pulse has a constant height and length, and information is stored in the pattern of pulses rather than in a single pulse. Every computer terminal is set up to send and receive this brand of message. Either by program or by UART (see Chapter 2), we send out a start pulse, eight information pulses, and one or two stop pulses. For a terminal, we let the 256 possible 8-bit patterns stand for the different letters and symbols we wish to type, but for sending analog information, we let them stand for values from zero through 255. The major advantage of PCM is noise immunity. Unless the noise converts a pulse all the way to a no-pulse or the other way around, the system just doesn't see the noise at all. For example, in Figure 12.8 it is still obvious that the signal being received was 1010, even though the noise is half as large as the signal. Of course, noise can get so large that it swamps out even this form of communication, but it's a lot better than simple amplitude modulation.

MULTIPLEXING

We have already discussed the situation in which we want to send more than one signal over a single communication path. Commercial radio solves this problem by sending the signals at different frequencies, and model radio controllers send pulses one after another in time. It is worthwhile to spend a page or two to pull these concepts together and to generalize them.

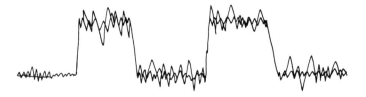

Figure 12.8 *A noisy pulse train.*

FREQUENCY MULTIPLEXING

Each information channel is assigned a separate frequency called its "subcarrier frequency." For four channels these subcarriers might be 1700 Hz, 1900 Hz, 2300 Hz, and 2900 Hz. The information to be conveyed on channel one is used to modulate subcarrier one (1700 Hz). This may be done by any of the above schemes: AM, FM, PDM, or PCM. Channel two information can modulate the second subcarrier using the same scheme as channel one (the usual case) or a different scheme if there is some valid reason to do so. After each subcarrier is modulated by its information, the subcarriers are added together, and this composite signal is used to modulate (by AM, FM, etc.) the main carrier.

At the receiver, the main carrier is detected and demodulated, and a set of narrow band-pass filters is used to separate the subcarriers, which are in turn demodulated, and the original information is recovered (see Figure 12.9). Filters can be expensive to build or buy, but each channel gets a continuous signal without problems due to sampling.

TIME-DIVISION MULTIPLEXING

A unit of time called a frame is divided up into successive slots. Channel 1 is given slot 1, channel 2 gets slot 2, and so forth. After the last channel is sent, there is usually a pause for resynching. During its time slot, a channel may send information in any way that seems good to it: AM, FM, etc. We looked at the case of pulse duration modulation, but the other methods have all been used. The device that switches between channels at the transmitter is called a "commutator," and the device that separates out the channels at the receiver is called a "decommutator." We saw how micros could be used for either or both. Time-division multiplexing is less cumbersome than frequency division, because it doesn't need a lot of narrow-band filters, but in the model radio scheme we looked at, the frame rate was 50 per second, so no input frequencies above 25 Hz could be allowed.

SPACE-DIVISION MULTIPLEXING

Finally, we should mention what a system is called if each channel of information gets its own communication channel. For example, channel 1 has a wire, channel 2 has a second wire, and so on. This is the simplest multiplexer and demultiplexer to build, but if the distances are great, it can eat up a lot of expensive copper wire, and if mobility is necessary, it can eat up a lot of the frequency spectrum. By symmetry with the above systems, this is called "space-division multiplexing."

THE ORGANIZATION OF BUSES

In the above sections, we have been considering the ways that one machine can talk to another. But what should be done if several machines want to hold a conversation? How do we keep them from all talking at once? How do we get the right messages to the right receivers?

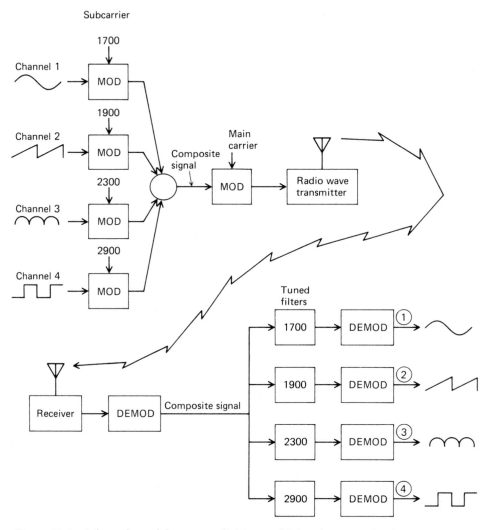

Figure 12.9 *A four-channel frequency division multiplexed communication system.*

Let us consider the following problem. We wish to make music, and we wish to do it in real time. We would like, for example, to be able to play four-part harmony, with each voice having a different timbre or quality. After a brief consideration, it becomes obvious that one microcomputer can't begin to do the job in real time.[*] Consider only a single 1000-Hz note. To get a reasonable approach to a sine wave or a triangular wave, we need at least 20 samples per period. That means no more than 50 microseconds to dredge up the sample value, output it, and get

---

[*]   Actually, there are programs commercially available to do just this on a single computer, but pretend you never heard of them.

ready to process the next value. Never mind deciding what basic frequency to use or anything about the other three notes with different wave shapes and different frequencies that have to be generated all at the same time. What we propose, then, is a set of five computers. One will act as the conductor, and the other four will each take a voice. One will play a square wave and sound rather like a bagpipe or oboe or other double-reed instrument. Number two will take the leading part with as good a sine wave as we can generate. This one will sound rather like a human whistle or a flute or piccolo. The third will generate a triangular-shaped wave form, which is an approximation to a clarinet, while the fourth will output a sawtooth, which some people think sounds like a violin. Not your average chamber ensemble, but one that will be fairly simple to program.

How can these five machines communicate among themselves? There are several reasonably diverse ways, and we will look at them all so that we can select the one most appropriate to our problem.

MULTIBUS

Each computer has four output ports and four input ports devoted to communication. Connections are as shown in Figure 12.10. We have a total of 20 communication paths. The number of pathways is equal to $N(N - 1)$, where N is the number of computers and is fine for two computers, just barely tolerable for five, and obviously impossible for 50. But the simplicity of operation is marvelous. When A wants to send a message to B, A puts it in the output port that leads to B.

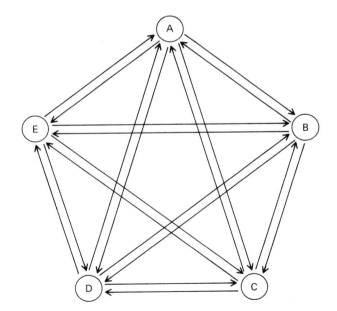

Figure 12.10 *Five computers with 20 communication paths.*

RING NETWORKS

To reduce the number of pathways and I/O ports, some multiple computer systems have been designed in a ring network a la Figure 12.11. If A wants to send a message to C, A sends the message to B with instructions to "pass it on." Actually, A puts a "header" on the message with the name of the destination in it. When a computer receives a message, it looks at the name of the destination. If not the ultimate addressee, the receiver sends the message on to the next computer. If that pathway is already in use, he may have to queue up the new message to wait its turn, but since A is the only one who may put a message on the AB pathway, there can be no "contention" for that pathway.

With this scheme, we have N computers and N pathways, which is as small a number of paths as you can get. The problem here is that messages may have to go through as many as $N - 2$ relay stations on their way to their destination. That has to eat up CPU time, so we have exchanged hardware (paths) for time (relays) in one of the classic computer design "compromises."

STAR NETWORK

A compromise between the speed of the multibus and the economy of the ring is a structure called a star (Figure 12.12). The computer in the center of the star spends most of its time handling communications for the other machines. To send a

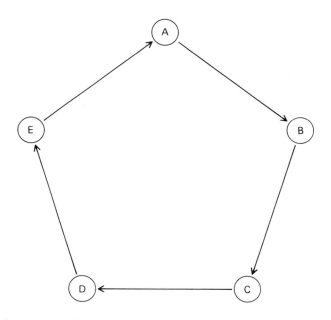

Figure 12.11   *A ring network.*

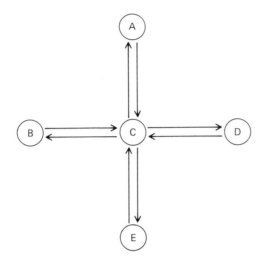

Figure 12.12 *A star network.*

message to D, A sends that message to C, who relays it to D. One relay gets your message to any other machine in the set, and for N machines there are

$$2 \cdot (N - 1)$$

pathways to establish. Once more, only one computer can talk on any given channel, so there is no competition for resources.

COMMON BUS

A common bus is defined as one to which more than one talker is connected (see Figure 12.13). A wants to send a message to B, and C wants to send a message to D. With only one set of hardware connecting all computers together, it is obvious that both conversations cannot go on at the same time, and that there must be some scheme for deciding who gets to talk when. The most obvious scheme is to time-multiplex the bus. Computer A gets slot 1 (from 12 to 12:05), B gets slot 2 (from 12:05 to 12:10), and so on. The problem with this is that if A doesn't have anything to say at this moment, A's time slot goes wasted and unused. This is a simple scheme but one that does not utilize its hardware to capacity; and that becomes a sin when many devices are competing for use of the bus.

One Master

If we can arrange it so that there is only one "master" of the bus, life again becomes simple. The master knows all and tells everyone—what to do. The master says, "A talk, B listen," and later says, "C talk, D listen." If A has a message to send to C, he must first get the master's attention and then his permission to use the bus. This might be done via a hierarchical interrupt scheme, such as we discussed in Chapter

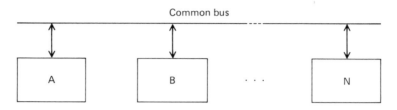

Figure 12.13 *A common bus.*

3. Each slave computer has a one-wire-wide pathway to the master, who scans all the incoming wires, selects the most deserving request, and awards the bus to that slave. This really looks a lot like the star network, except that once the master lends the bus to a slave, the slave may then use it as his own until it gets taken away again.

Common Bus without an Arbitrator

It is possible to design a common bus system without an arbitrator or bus master. The design is moderately complex but is worth going through because of the principles involved. A symbolic diagram of one station is shown in Figure 12.14. Across the top of the diagram we have the address and data lines, and it is the control of these lines that the rest of the diagram is concerned with.

    All units that wish to use the bus are given a priority by the way in which their "control stations" are chained together. The station at the left end of the chain has the highest priority, and that at the right end of the chain has the lowest. Whatever theoretical scheme may be chosen for determining priority, whether 17 distinct levels or something else, in the end it comes down to "who gets the nod after a dead heat?" and that means A is either above or below B. No other solution is possible. Therefore a single priority chain may be inelegant, but it is a perfectly general solution. (A little later we will describe how a CPU can appear at several places on the priority chain.)

    Each bus station has one flip-flop, three gates, and a leading edge detector devoted to bus control. Operation is as follows: The present user of the bus finishes work and issues a "Bus Release" signal, which consists of a pulse. Suppose the station we are looking at in Figure 12.14 wants the bus. Then the "I want the bus" line will be high, and when the leading edge detector (LEDD) sees the rising edge of the Bus Release signal, gate A passes that signal through to *set* the flip-flop to the ARMED position. The signal from the flip-flop saying that this station is ARMED goes through the OR circuit of gate B and passes down the chain to all stations to the right as BUS BUSY. As the signal goes down the chain, it resets (turns off) any ARMED flip-flops it may encounter. Thus we end up with the leftmost station desiring the bus in the ARMED state and everybody else disarmed. The Bus Release signal lasts long enough for everybody to get disarmed, except the station with the highest priority, and when the Bus Release signal drops back to zero, gate

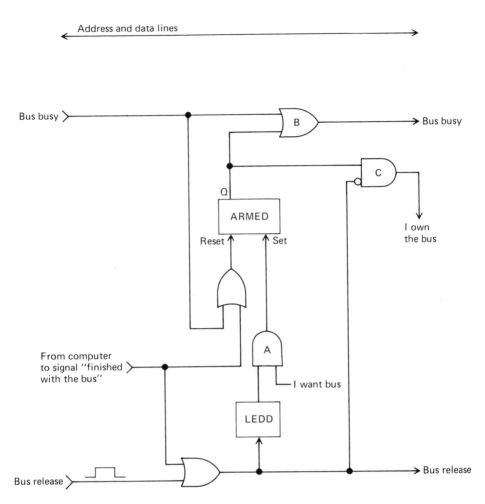

Figure 12.14 *One station of a common bus without an arbitrator.*

C opens, generating the signal that this station now owns the bus. The station uses the bus, and when it is done, it resets its ARMED flip-flop, dropping the Bus Busy line to zero, and then generates a Bus Release pulse.

The reason for the fairly complicated scheme is to ensure that only one station at a time grabs the bus by separating the "time of request" (the leading edge of the Bus Release) from the "time of action" (the trailing edge of the Bus Release pulse). Nobody can get ARMED after the time of request, and there is plenty of time provided to allow all except the leftmost ARMED station to be reset.

There is a small problem with the above design. Suppose nobody wants the bus when the present owner releases it? Then there will be no new owner and nobody to ever release it again. We can solve this problem and also simplify each individual station by adding an "idiot box" at the right end of the chain. This "idiot box" watches the Bus Busy line, and whenever that falls to zero (indicating that the present owner has disarmed itself), the idiot box begins repeating "Bus Release! Bus Release!" over and over until the Bus Busy line goes up to one (indicating that somebody has taken the bus). Each station can become simpler, because it does not have to generate the Bus Release signal. It just resets the ARMED flip-flop, and the idiot box takes care of the rest.

Exercise 12.1: Bus Control

To demonstrate to yourself that you understand all of this discussion, write a program for a microcomputer that will duplicate this behavior in the control of a 16-bit-address-plus-8-bit-data bus. You will need 1-bit input from your "left" (Bus Busy IN), 1-bit output to your "right" (Bus Busy OUT), three 8-bit tri-state ports to actually control the bus, and one more input bit to sample the "bus release" line. Figure 12.15 shows an outline of the system. Port A is the bus control port, B and C are the address ports, and D is the data port. A_7 is the input from the left, A_0 is the output to the right, and bit A_6 is used to test for a bus release signal.

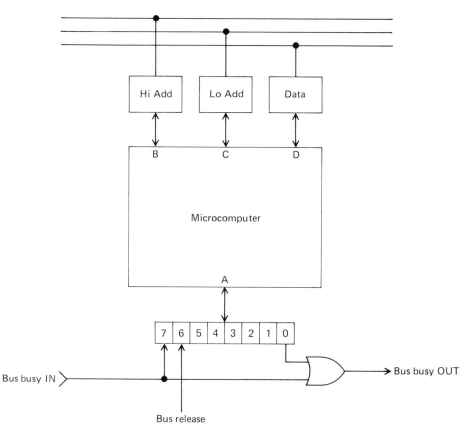

Figure 12.15 *A microcomputer set up to control a bus—assuming an "idiot box" to generate a bus release signal.*

The OR circuit on the Bus Busy line means that the computer doesn't have to spend all its time updating that line and may actually have a chance to do some computing.

A good protocol would be for a micro to wait until the bus release line is zero before trying to get control of the bus. That way it won't jump into the middle of a control sequence and screw up everybody's timing. Sometimes a CPU may need to assume different priorities, depending on what program it is carrying out. The easiest way to implement this on a masterless bus, such as the above, is to give the CPU three or four stations strategically located along the chain of devices, and to allow it to raise an "I want the bus" line in any one of these, depending on what priority level it is running at.

THE MUSIC MASTER

Let's turn back to the problem that got us started on multiple computers and their connections, namely, the problem of four-part harmony. The first thing to realize is that the players have nothing to say to the conductor. Given that, it seems that the best way to organize this system is for the conductor to tell each player what frequency to generate and how loud it should be and to rely on the player to do its job. Duration of a note can be handled by the conductor telling the player to stop playing or to change notes as appropriate. Each player will generate its own wave form at the frequency and intensity decreed by the conductor. If we like, we can give each player its own D to A converter and power amplifier and speaker so that the sound can come from the four corners of the room. If that seems too expensive, we can combine the output of the four D to A converters in a resistive adder network (see Figure 12.16).

We can go even further and add up the numbers in digital form and then convert only once from digital to analog. Figure 12.17 shows this approach. The sixth computer, called the "producer," samples the outputs of the four players as fast as it can and outputs the sum of those signals on the one DAC to the power amplifier

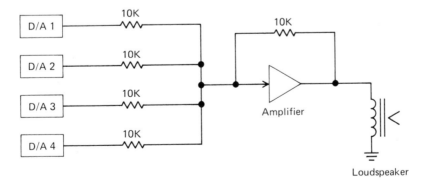

Figure 12.16 *An adder network to sum up the outputs of the four players and present the composite signal to the amplifier.*

and loudspeaker. Since everybody is friendly in this organization, the players will
output numbers in the range of 0 to 63, so the producer merely has to add the four
ports to get a number in the range of 0–255, which it can store directly in the output port without having to do a divide or a shift right to keep from overflowing.
After we have looked at how much work the producer and the conductor have to
do, we can see whether or not we could make them be the same machine.

The Producer

We'll start with the producer. Given ports P_1, P_2, P_3, and P_4 as input and P_5 as output, all it needs to do is

LOAD:	INPUT	P1
	STA	TEMP 1
	INPUT	P2
	STA	TEMP 2
	INPUT	P3
	STA	TEMP 3
	INPUT	P4
	ADD	TEMP 1
	ADD	TEMP 2
	ADD	TEMP 3
	OUTPUT	P5
	JMP	LOAD

which will take something like 25 microseconds to accomplish. This means a
Nyquist frequency of 20,000 Hz. We could probably cut that down to 10,000 Hz or
even 5000 without serious loss. That would give us 50 to 100 microseconds per
loop, which might be enough to do the conducting in.

The Player

The players are going to obtain their notes from the conductor. After some little
thought, we modestly present the code of Figure 12.18 for the players. We have
three tables called VALUE, LARGE, and SMALL. VALUE has sixteen entries in it
and by these entries determines the magnitude of the number the player will put
out. For a maximum-amplitude square wave these numbers would be: 0, 0, 0, 0, 0,
0, 0, 0, 63, 63, 63, 63, 63, 63, 63, 63 (decimal). A sawtooth wave would have
values: 0, 3, 7, . . . , 59, 63 (decimal). Once each cycle the player will run through
these 16 values, outputting each in turn.

   Each player will be able to play three full octaves. At concert pitch, middle C
(otherwise known as C_4) is 261.64 vibrations per second; C_5 is 523.28 vps, and C_3
= 130.82, while C_2 = 65.41. In the 1911 microseconds that elapse per complete
vibration of C_5, we want to put out 16 values, so we must allow 119.43
microseconds for each value. Three octaves down we must allow 955.5
microseconds between value changes.

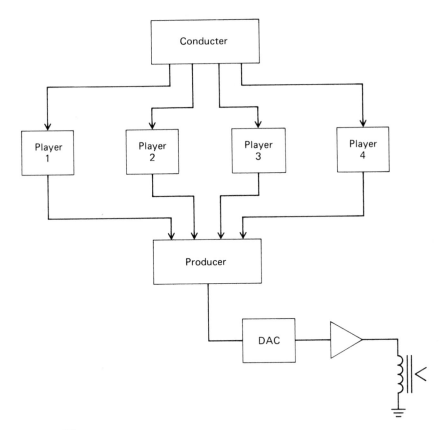

Figure 12.17 *The six-computer concert.*

The smallest possible difference between two durations generated by our computer will be one microsecond (naturally different machines will have different clock rates). Not that we can get an instruction executed in that amount of time, but we can get a pair of loops that differ by just that much. Loops L_1 and L_2 of Figure 12.18 are such loops with delays that differ by one microsecond.

The conductor sends the player a positive number X, which the player interprets as being the name of a note. (Negative numbers represent rests and instructions on changing intensity.) Using X, the player looks up in the table LARGE (at the Xth entry) how many 6-microsecond loops to execute, and then in table SMALL (at the Xth entry) how many 5-microsecond loops. There never need to be more than four of the longer loops.

Take the generation of note C_3 with 478 microseconds per value. The basic code with no repeats of either L_1 or L_2 takes 44 microseconds. This leaves $478 - 44 = 438$ microseconds to be used up in L_1 and L_2. Looping 87 times around L_2 will eat up $87 \times 5 = 435$ microseconds. If we go 86 times around L_2 and once around L_1, we use up an extra microsecond. Three times around L_1 and 84 times around L_2 give $6 \times 3 + 84 \times 5 = 438$ microseconds. So in the LARGE and SMALL entries that correspond to C_3 we will store 3 and 84.

```
BEGIN:    INPUT      IOPORT        Get the note to play from the conductor.
          BMA        CONTROL       It is a command.
          STA        NOTE          Hold it in NOTE.
          LDX        POINTER       This tells which value to
                                   put out next.
          LDAX       VALUE         Get size from table of values.
          OUTPUT     SPEAKER
          INX                      Increment pointer.
          TXA
          SUBIM      16
          BMA        DELAY         Pointer <16.
          LDAIM      0             Pointer ≥16.
DELAY:    STA        POINTER       Save pointer for next time.
          LDX        NOTE          Get the name of the note to play.
          LDAX       LARGE         How many large loops?
   L1:    SUB        ONE           This loop takes
          BNA        L1            6 microseconds.
          LDAX       SMALL
   L2:    SUBIM      1             This loop takes
          BNA        L2            5 microseconds.
          JMP        BEGIN         Do it all again.
ONE:      .BYT       1
```

Figure 12.18 *Basic timing loop for a player, accurate to one microsecond.*

Using the above scheme, we can adjust each delay to within one microsecond, which is, at most, one percent of the delay required for C_5. A somewhat more accurate scheme might let Y (the index pointing to the value) be as shown for values from 0 to 14, but on 15, the last value before starting over, one could jump to some additional code that took its delays from tables LAST LARGE and LAST SMALL. These could be adjusted to bring the duration of the complete period of the note (all 16 values) to within one microsecond of the decimal amount—roughly one part in 2000, which would be considerably "truer" in tone.

What control functions might the conductor send over? To begin with, he might say "shut up for a while." This is technically called a "rest." He might also tell the player to play louder or softer. Each player could store a number of tables of values. A very loud sawtooth might be 0, 3, 7, . . . , 59, 63 whereas a very quiet sawtooth might be 24, 25, 26, . . . , 38, 39—again centered around 32, the midpoint in the range from 0 to 63. Rather than moving tables of values around, the reader might like to consider indirect addressing as a solution to the varying intensity problem.

The Conductor

The conductor has to have a copy of the music broken down into four parts. For very fast music, he might expect to have to tell a player a new note every 64th of a second. If the note is staccato, that will mean a rest between each note or a new command every 8 milliseconds for each player. A long note might last as much as a second. For each player the conductor will have a string of notes and information as to how long those notes should be sustained. This is called the SCORE, and a conductor must know the score, so we have been told. Two bytes per note per player will be required. We can store the duration of the note in multiples of 8 milliseconds. This gives us notes as long as 2 seconds if we require them (256 × 8 ≃ 2000 milliseconds).

Each time a timer counts out 8 milliseconds, the conductor will look at each player and see if the note that player is playing is finished yet, and if not, he will subtract one from the number of intervals yet to go. If the note is over, the conductor will get a new note and new duration for this player. Clearly, this can be done with ease in the 8 milliseconds that must elapse before it has to be done all again.

FOLDING THE CONDUCTOR

Let's see if we can save a CPU and make the sound producer and the conductor reside in a single machine. Assuming a 50-microsecond period for the producer, we have approximately half of the CPU time available for things other than reading in the output values of the four players. The problem is that this time is broken up into small chunks punctuated every 50 microseconds by the need to get a new set of values for the output.

Now, one of the nice things about programming under tight time constraints such as we have here is that it offers an excuse for discarding all the pious platitudes we have been taught about structured programming; about one-in, one-out, about top-down approaches and all that sort of jazz. We want to warn you that each time you relax one of the constraints of good programming practice, you should be fully aware of the bargain you are making. In exchange for a couple of microseconds of execution time, you will probably pay (averaged out over a lifetime) an hour of your time in debugging and a half hour of somebody else's time trying to figure out what you did. (We made these numbers up, but they feel about right.) So do it when you have to, but don't forget that the jolliest of pipers has children in need of new shoes.

So with that warning in mind, how can we meld the producer, who has a reasonably short task to perform quite often, with the conductor, who has a reasonably long task to perform relatively infrequently? What we will do is break up the conductor's job into a number of pieces and layer these pieces with instances of the producer like a multideck sandwich. The conductor's job separates naturally to update one player at a time.

We will set up a timer to wait until it is time to begin a new cycle of conducting. We gather our outputs from the players (called "gather" hereafter), and then we check an 8-millisecond timer for time out. If it is still running, we delay until 50 microseconds are up and then go back to the beginning again (see Figure 12.19).

If the 8-millisecond timer has timed out, we drop into a section of code called NOTE-0, followed by NOTE-1, NOTE-2, etc. (see Figure 12.20). NOTE-0 restarts

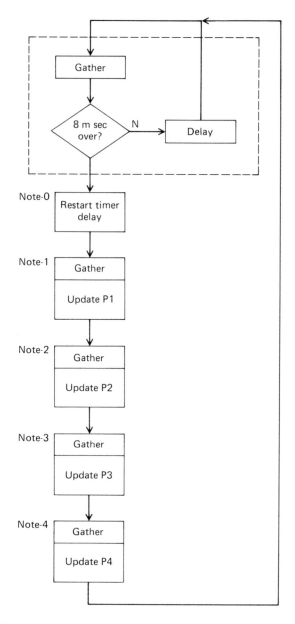

Figure 12.19 *The flow diagram for the combined conductor-producer.*

the timer and then idles until time to do another "gather." NOTE-1 (see Figure 12.20) does the gather and then decrements the counter called ONETIME. If it is not zero—if there is still more duration left for this note—it jumps off to SKIP-1 to idle until time for the next "gather." If the note is over, the code will get a new note from the table called ONENOTE and put it out to player 1, and a new duration from table ONEDUE and store it in ONETIME. Each player has his own pair of tables (up to 256 entries) for notes and their duration and his own pointer into these tables. By maximum use of page zero addressing, we managed to keep this code to 33 microseconds and with the time to gather of 20 microseconds can maintain a 53-microsecond gathering schedule. We were aiming for 50, so this isn't really too bad. Suppose it was? Then we would break each little updating piece of code into two parts and insert gathers (and delays as required) between them.

We could actually have kept to 50 microseconds by moving the SKIP instructions off to some other place where we wouldn't have had to jump over them. I didn't think it was worth it for a mere three microseconds.

SHARING PORTS

As we have arranged things above, the conductor-producer has two ports connecting him to each player, and he is either talking on one or listening on the other—never both at once. In fact, he is only really communicating with one player at a time. The mingy and the pennypinching will already be plotting how to save by using only a single port for all the communications that have to be done. Before jumping into that, let us take an initial dip and examine how the conductor-producer could talk to one player over a single port. The problem, of course, is turning the communication path around so that first the conductor can talk and then the player can talk. Moreover, they will need to shake hands on each transaction.

We suppose that both parties have 6520s or their equivalents. Since the producer must read more often than the conductor must send a new note, the line should normally be left running from the player to the conductor-producer. Naturally, the player will have to store internally the note he is playing and not rely on finding it in the input port.

The conductor discovers that it is time to send a new note to the player. He makes his port be output, puts the new note in it, and sends an interrupt to the player. The player sees the interrupt, makes his port be input, reads the new note, makes his port be output again, and sends a response to the conductor via the player's I_2 line, which is connected to the conductor's I_1 line. When the conductor sees his I_1 line wag, he knows that the player has received the signal, and he can make his port be input again. How long will all this take, and can we keep the gathering rhythm? Look just at what the player has to do in Figure 12.21. First of all, it takes at least 6 microseconds to respond to an interrupt. Then the player has to make the control register point at the direction register, so that can be accessed to make it say "input." Then switch the pointer back to the data register and read the note. Next we have to make the control register point to the direction register again, so we can switch back to output, point at the data register, and restore the output word. Even if all this doesn't screw up the basic timing loops—which it will—it is clearly too long to fit between gathers, and it will be rather hard to do a gather with the port turned the wrong way. Conclusion: Don't use a 6520 if you have to turn it around in a hurry.

```
BASELOOP:    LDA      PLAYER-1  ⎫
             ADD      PLAYER-2  ⎪
             ADD      PLAYER-3  ⎬   Gather.
             ADD      PLAYER-4  ⎪
             STA      OUTPUT    ⎭
             LDA      TIMER         Read timer.
             BZA      NOTE-0
             JSR      WASTE-24      Delay until time to restart.
             JMP      BASELOOP
NOTE-0:      LDAIM    CONST         Set the timer constant to
             STA      TIMER         restart the timer.
             JSR      WASTE-20
NOTE-1:      LDA      PLAYER-1  ⎫
             ADD      PLAYER-2  ⎪
             ADD      PLAYER-3  ⎬   Gather.
             ADD      PLAYER-4  ⎪
             STA      OUTPUT    ⎭
             DEC      ONE-TIME      Is note for P-1 over yet?
             BNA      SKIP-1
             INC      ONE-PTR       Yes, bump index I.
             LDX      ONE-PTR
             LDAX     ONE-NOTE      Get new note.
             STA      PORT-1        Output note to port 1.
             LDAX     ONE-DUR       Set new duration.
             STA      ONE-TIME
             JMP      NOTE-2
SKIP-1:      JSR      WASTE-12
NOTE-2:      .
             .
             .
```

Figure 12.20 *Baseloop code and code for updating player 1 for the conductor-producer. Assumes memory-mapped I/O ports.*

Can we break the problem up another way? Can we, for example, do all the output from the conductor on one port and all the input on a second? Let's see.

The sign bit will again be used to signal control information. A message sent out from the conductor will consist of two bytes. Byte 1 will be negative; byte 2 will be positive. Byte 1 will contain (in the low-order two bits) the name of the player to whom the message is addressed. When the conductor wants to send a new note to player 2, he puts the word $82 in the outbound port. All players examine their input ports at each value change (see Figure 12.18). When a negative word appears in the input port, each player jumps off to his CONTROL code to decide if the message is for him. If not, he goes back to playing his current note. If the message is for him, the player tells the conductor he is paying attention by raising bit 6 of the port (always output for the players and input for the conductor) to

```
        LDAIM    $00           Set the switch to point to the
        STA      CTLREG        direction register.
        LDAIM    $00           Make direction register say "input."
        STA      DIRREG
        LDAIM    $04           Set to point to Data.
        STA      CTLREG
        LDA      DATAREG       Capture the note
        STA      NOTE          and save it.
        LDAIM    $00           Set CTL to point to direction register
        STA      CTLREG        and send "ack" on I₂ to conductor.
        LDAIM    $FF           Make direction register
        STA      DIRREG        say "output."
        LDAIM    $04           Point at data register.
        STA      CTLREG
        LDA      OUTPUT        Refresh the value
        STA      DATAREG       in the output register.
```

Figure 12.21 *Turning the player's port through 360 degrees. Assumes memory-addressed ports and control registers in a 6520-type PIA.*

one. The conductor now removes the address byte (the negative one) and outputs the information byte with bit 7 equal to zero. The player sees the sign bit change, reads in the information from bits 5–0 of the port, and tells the conductor he has the information by dropping bit 6 to zero. The conductor sees this drop and can now send a new message to another player.

If the lowest note a player can play is C_2 and there are 16 values per cycle, the longest delay before a player gets around to noticing that a message is for him will be 956 microseconds. The handshaking described above might stretch out over another 50 or 100 microseconds, so worst-case time to change all four players' notes would be under 5 milliseconds, or less than a 200th of a second. A full symphony orchestra spreads over a width of 50 feet or more, and the sound waves from one side of the hall will take about 50 milliseconds to reach the opposite side. This delay is less than a tenth of that, so it seems tolerable.

The players' code will be fairly straightforward. When they get a command addressed to somebody else, they just jump back and continue as if nothing had happened. Timing might be a bit messy, but we can handle that. When the message is for him, the player is going to change behavior, so delays will be irrelevant until he starts a new note. The conductor's code will be somewhat harder to write, because he has to do all this code between gatherings and without losing the rhythm. But we have already seen how to do that, so we know it can be handled.

How about sharing the player-to-producer bus? I say no. Once every 50 or so microseconds you would have to get each player's attention, shake hands with him, and transfer a byte of information. Much too complicated to do in software. Can hardware help? Sure! Put in four buses! Short of that, we can reduce the number of ports from $2N$ to $N + 2$ by the scheme described in Figure 12.22. This is

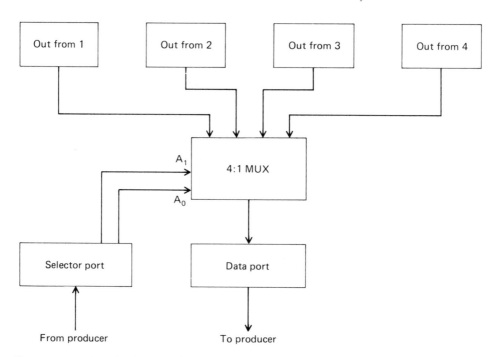

Figure 12.22 *A multiplexed bus for gathering information.*

scarcely dramatic for $N = 4$ but improves as N gets large. We add a four-to-one multiplexer and a selector output port on the producer. The producer puts a number in the selector port that corresponds to the player he wishes to hear from. The MUX sees this number on address lines $A_1 A_0$ and connects the appropriate port to its output, which is then read by the producer. Each player maintains an up-to-date value in his output port at all times, so nobody needs to rush around capturing anybody's attention. Unfortunately, the code, as shown in Figure 12.23, takes so long (47 microseconds) that in order to keep up a 50-microsecond gathering rhythm, we need a full-time computer for the producer and another for the conductor. Hardly a good trade: two ports for a multiplexer and a computer. Still, I suppose we had to look and see.

DIRECT MEMORY ACCESS

There is another way for two processors to communicate with each other. It is called DMA, or Direct Memory Access. The original purpose of DMA was to allow a fast disk to do a block transfer without continually interrupting the CPU. In a sense that's our problem, too, so let's look at the mechanism.

When the disk (read "other processor") wants access to memory, it raises (or lowers, depending on the sense of the logic) a line called a "processor wait" line. As

```
BEGIN:    INC    SELECTOR       Add 1 to number in the port
          LDA    DATAPORT       controlling the multiplexer.
          INC    SELECTOR
          ADD    DATAPORT
          INC    SELECTOR
          ADD    DATAPORT
          INC    SELECTOR
          ADD    DATAPORT
          STA    OUTPUT
          JMP    BEGIN
```

Figure 12.23 *Code for a producer using the circuitry of Figure 12.22. Assumes memory-mapped I/O and the ability to increment a memory address (INC SELECTOR).*

soon as the present memory cycle is over, the processor goes into a "wait" state and releases control of the memory address lines and data pathway lines. That is to say it has tri-state output, and while "waiting" it "floats" the address and data lines. The processor also raises a line sometimes called the "wait acknowledge" line, which the DMA hardware can see.

When it sees the wait acknowledge, the DMA hardware puts an address on the address lines, data on the data lines, and a "write" signal on the read/write control line. When the memory signals that it has captured the data, the DMA hardware releases the bus lines and then releases the processor wait line. The CPU takes up where it left off, which may have been in the middle of an instruction, and goes on its way, never knowing that the DMA hardware crept in and then crept out again. This procedure is sometimes called "cycle stealing" for this very reason.

This approach can be extended, and we can imagine our five processors grouped around a common pot of memory, taking turns dipping their fingers in to read or write data in one of eight different cells labeled C-to-p1, C-to-p2, C-to-p3, C-to-p4, p1-to-C, p2-to-C, p3-to-C and p4-to-C. But I have a feeling we are getting out of the area of using computers and drifting into the area of designing them.

Lots of music is written in four-part harmony. In particular, I am fond of an old book entitled *Barber Shop Ballads and How to Sing Them,* by Sigmund Spaeth, published by Prentice-Hall in 1940. If your taste runs more to classical or rock, you'll have to find your own sources, but plenty of them exist.

Appendix
A Description
of Our
Hypothetical
Machine

In order to make this book understandable to the largest possible number of readers, we have written what code we needed for a hypothetical machine that does not exist and probably never will. This machine is a single-address machine with one index register (X), one accumulator (A), a stack pointer (SP), a vectored interrupt controlled by an interrupt-inhibit bit (I), and the provision of input and output ports and three addressing modes.

The addressing modes are as follows:

- Immediate addressing

  LDAIM α The number α stored in the instruction is loaded into the accumulator.

- Direct addressing

  LDA α The number stored in memory location α is loaded into the accumulator.

- Indexed addressing

  LDAX α The effective address is formed by adding the contents of the index register X to α. Then the contents of the memory location pointed to by the effective address are loaded into the accumulator.

The following group of instructions may use all three addressing modes.

LDA	Load the accumulator.
LDX	Load the index register.
ADD	Add the value to the accumulator.
SUB	Subtract the value from the accumulator.
AND	Logical AND of value with the accumulator.
IOR	Logical inclusive OR of value with the accumulator.

182

The next group of instructions may be direct or indexed but not immediate.

STA	Store contents of accumulator at effective address.
INC	Add 1 to the number stored at the effective address. Does not change the accumulator.
DEC	Subtract 1 from the number stored at the effective address. Does not change the accumulator.
JMP	Put the effective address into the program counter.
JSR	Save the old contents of the program counter on the stack, and then put the effective address into the program counter.
BZA	If the contents of the accumulator are zero, put the effective address into the program counter.
BNA	If the contents of the accumulator are nonzero, put the effective address into the program counter.
BPA	If the contents of the accumulator are positive (≥ 0), put the effective address into the program counter.
BMA	If the contents of the accumulator are minus (<0), put the effective address into the program counter.

The input and output instructions permit direct addressing only.

INPUT α	Copy the 8-bit byte from port α into the accumulator, right-justified.
OUTPUT α	Copy the low 8 bits of the accumulator to output port α.

Last we have a group of instructions that use no address at all.

SEI	Set the interrupt-inhibit bit to 1, preventing interrupts.
CLI	Clear the interrupt-inhibit bit to 0, allowing interrupts to occur.
RTI	Return from interrupt by loading the program counter from the stack and clearing the I bit.
HLT	Stop the computer and wait for the user to push the start button.
INX	Add 1 to the contents of the index register.
ASR	Shift the contents of the accumulator right one position. Sign bit is replicated in bit 6, and old contents of bit 0 are lost.
TXA	Copy the contents of the X register into the accumulator.
TAX	Copy the contents of the accumulator to the index register.
PUSHA	Push a copy of the contents of the accumulator onto the stack.
PUSHX	Push a copy of the contents of the index register onto the stack.
POPA	Remove the top item from the stack, and put it in the accumulator.
POPX	Remove the top item from the stack, and put it in the index register.

Any practical computer would need many other instructions in order to function properly. We have included here only those we had occasion to use in the text.

Two memory locations are reserved for the interrupt system. They are:

IRQVEC   A reserved location used to hold the address of the routine that will handle IRQ interrupts. Must be loaded by programmer.

NMIVEC   The same for NMI interrupts.

If the I-bit is 0 and the IRQ is at 0, an IRQ interrupt will be generated. Three things happen:

1.   The old value in the program counter is saved on the stack.

2.   The interrupt-inhibit bit I is set to 1.

3.   The contents of IRQVEC are loaded into the program counter.

Regardless of the state of the I-bit, when the NMI line *goes* to zero, an NMI interrupt will be generated. Action is the same as for an IRQ interrupt, except that the program counter will be loaded with the contents of NMIVEC.

Index*

---

* You'll get around in this index very well if you note the following ground rules:

1. Nothing comes before something, so you'll find "mass" before "mass-spring-damper."
2. Punctuation marks come before letters, so you'll find "D-flip-flop" before DAC.
3. A number is listed under the spelling of its first word. Look for "488 bus" under F.
4. If you want to know more about an ADC, for instance, also scan the pages following p. 73.

185